A Wild Sort of Beauty

Public Places and Private Visions

Essay by

Robert L. McGrath

The Adirondack Museum
Blue Mountain Lake, New York

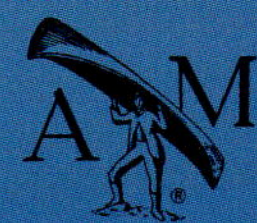

ii

Exhibition:
The Adirondack Museum
May 23 - October 15, 1992

Exhibit and Project Director   Caroline Mastin Welsh
Catalogue Editor   Alice Wolf Gilborn
Checklist Editor   Tracy Nelson Meehan

Copyright © 1992 by the Adirondack Museum

Library of Congress Catalog Card Number: 92-71408
International Standard Book Number: 0-910020-43-4

Catalogue Design by WilliamPadgettDesign, Erieville, New York
The typeface used throughout this publication is Adobe Garamond. The page layout software was QuarkXpress® 3.1 with a Macintosh IIfx computer.

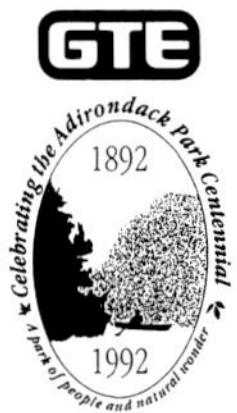

The printing of this catalogue was made possible through the generosity of GTE. Published May 20, 1992, by the Adirondack Museum of the Adirondack Historical Association in honor of the Centennial of the Adirondack Park.

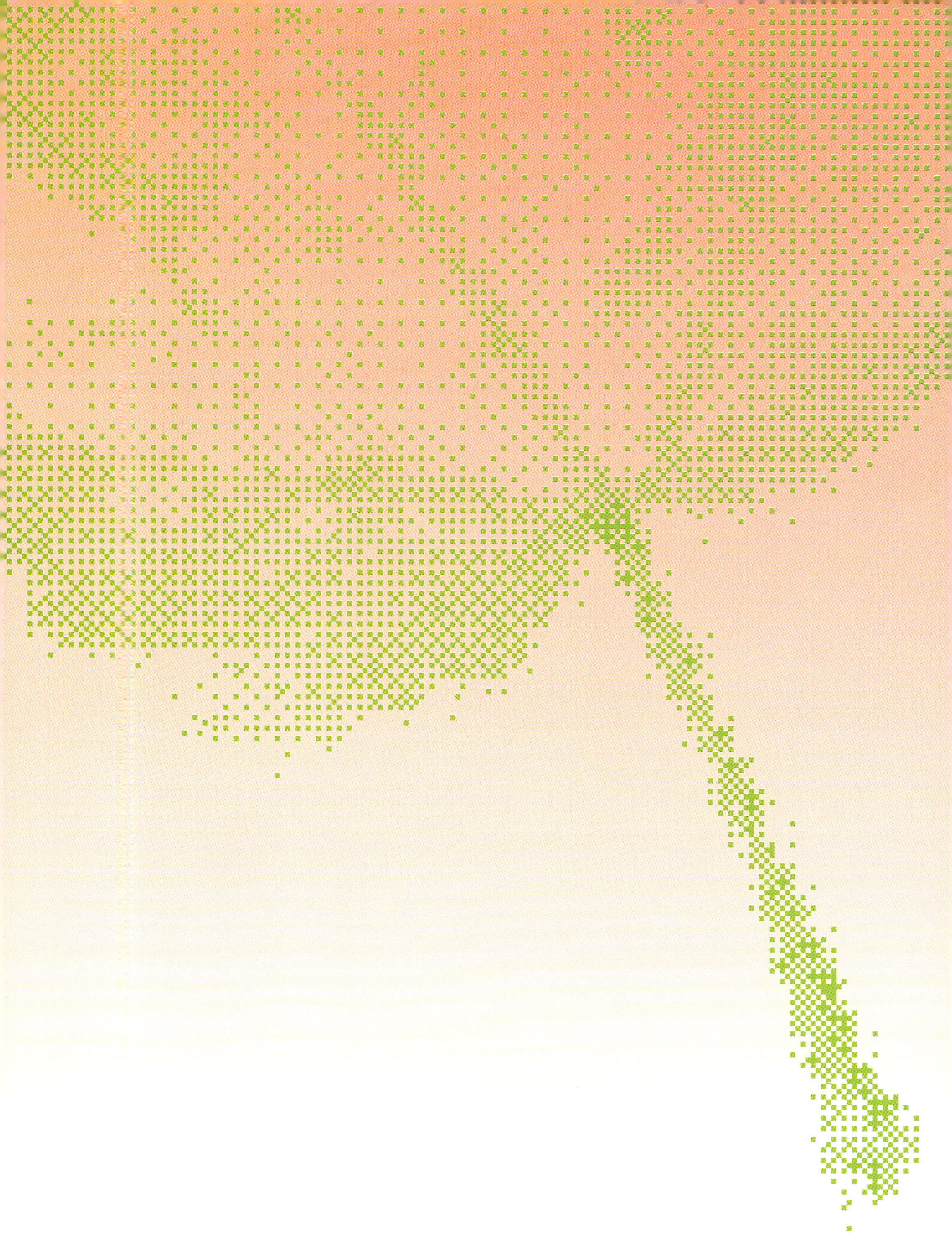

PREFACE

N 1837 THOMAS COLE, ACCOMPANIED BY HIS friend and fellow artist Asher B. Durand, described the country around Schroon Lake: "The scenery is not grand, but has a wild sort of beauty that approaches it: quietness—solitude—the untamed—the unchanged aspect of nature—an aspect which the scene has worn thousands of years.... Here we felt the sublimity of untamed wilderness, and the majesty of the eternal mountains."

To English-born Cole, America's most distinctive characteristic was its wildness, as was found in the rugged mountain wilderness of upstate New York. Well before Cole's sojourn in the Adirondacks, artists had painted the Catskills and White Mountains, but because of this region's inaccessibility, it was not until the middle of the 19th century that artists, other than Thomas Cole and Charles Ingham, came to capture the Adirondacks in paint. For nearly 150 years, pictorial views of this "wild sort of beauty," which is now the Adirondack Park, have been changing, from Thomas Cole's evocation of sublimity to Frank Owen's contemporary and abstract reintegration of nature, man and politics. In turn, these artistic renditions of wilderness have structured popular 19th and 20th century consciousness of the Adirondacks as a place, and of nature and wilderness as a concept.

Artistic visions, informed by a complex of cultural notions, packaged the Adirondack as well as the American Wilderness in a multitude of images of water, woods and mountains. As early as 1835 Thomas Cole decried the destruction of the American landscape. In the very civilizing of the land, nature is threatened or destroyed. Cole notes in his "Complaint of the Forest": "We feed ten-thousand fires! In one short day/The woodland growth of centuries is consumed...." His concern was echoed by naturalists like George Perkins Marsh, Verplanck Colvin, S.H. Hammond and artists like Julian Rix. Businessmen joined the cry when destruction of water resources in the Adirondacks and Catskills threatened downstate canal interests. Legislation to set aside the Adirondacks as a Park—a public place of wilderness— was signed May 20, 1892. The awakening of this national consciousness of natural place—of the significance of environment and man's relationship to it—began, in large part, with the landscape artists. One hundred years after the Park was created, we can still see the "unchanged aspect of nature" and "the majesty of the eternal mountains" the landscapists strove to capture and interpret.

The centennial anniversary of the creation of the Adirondack Park by the New York State Legislature is an occasion celebrated throughout the Adirondacks by exhibitions, lectures, outings, symposia, publications, fairs and musical events. Planning for these activities began in 1990 with the incorporation of the Committee for the 1992 Adirondack Park Centennial. Committee Chair Barbara McMartin's indefatigable energy and inspiration provided the spur for most of the events and the Adirondack Museum's exhibit "'A Wild Sort of Beauty': Public Places and Private Visions" is no exception.

The exhibition and catalogue were made possible by many people: Director Craig Gilborn's support and commitment and the devotion to the project by Guest Curator Robert L. McGrath, Professor of Art History at Dartmouth College, were paramount. Museum Registrar Tracy Meehan provided museum Curator and Co-curator of the exhibit, Caroline Welsh, invaluable assistance with loan negotiations and compiled the checklist. Other members of the Curatorial department cheerfully assisted with the myriad of details necessary to accomplish the task. Museum Editor Alice Gilborn edited the catalogue essay as well as supervised its production. We are grateful to Graphic Designer William Padgett for his graceful and responsive design as well as his timeliness. The printing of the exhibition catalogue was made possible by the generosity of GTE to whom the museum and the Centennial Committee are indebted for their willing support.

Last, but by no means least, we wish to thank all our lenders whose generosity has enriched this Centennial exhibition. Without their cooperation the scope of the exhibit would not have been possible.

CAROLINE M. WELSH

Curator of Exhibits and Paintings

A Central Park for the World:

Nature and Self in the
Adirondacks

DON NICE
Adirondack Totem
1990
Oil on canvas
80 x 43
Collection of the artist.

I N PROTRAYING THE ADIRONDACKS AS AN ENLARGED urban park, an unknown 19th century *New York Times* reporter employed a metaphor that defined the north country from a cosmopolitan perspective.[1] In the deepest sense, the region has never been understood apart from the city. From first to last, metropolitan values have given shape to the wilderness, as private visions have engaged these public places in a complex and everchanging social and political dialogue.[2] Residing, however, in the opposition to culture, the human desire for nature is perennially mediated by the structures of art.

As moderns we find in nature what we bring to nature. The landscape as such is a physical constant upon which we project our shifting cultural ideals. Art, in turn, does not reflect reality, but in fact constructs reality for the viewer. A recent painting (Fig. 1) by the "pop-realist" Don Nice not only confirms this thesis but alludes suggestively to over two hundred years of creative contact between American artists and the Adirondack north woods of New York State. At the center of Nice's monumental canvas a waterfall enclosed by a circle denotes the cycle of nature and its enduring perfection. Above the sphere of nature a bear, enframed by an isosceles triangle, symbolizes the domain of wild animals, while at the base of the composition objects of everyday life such as

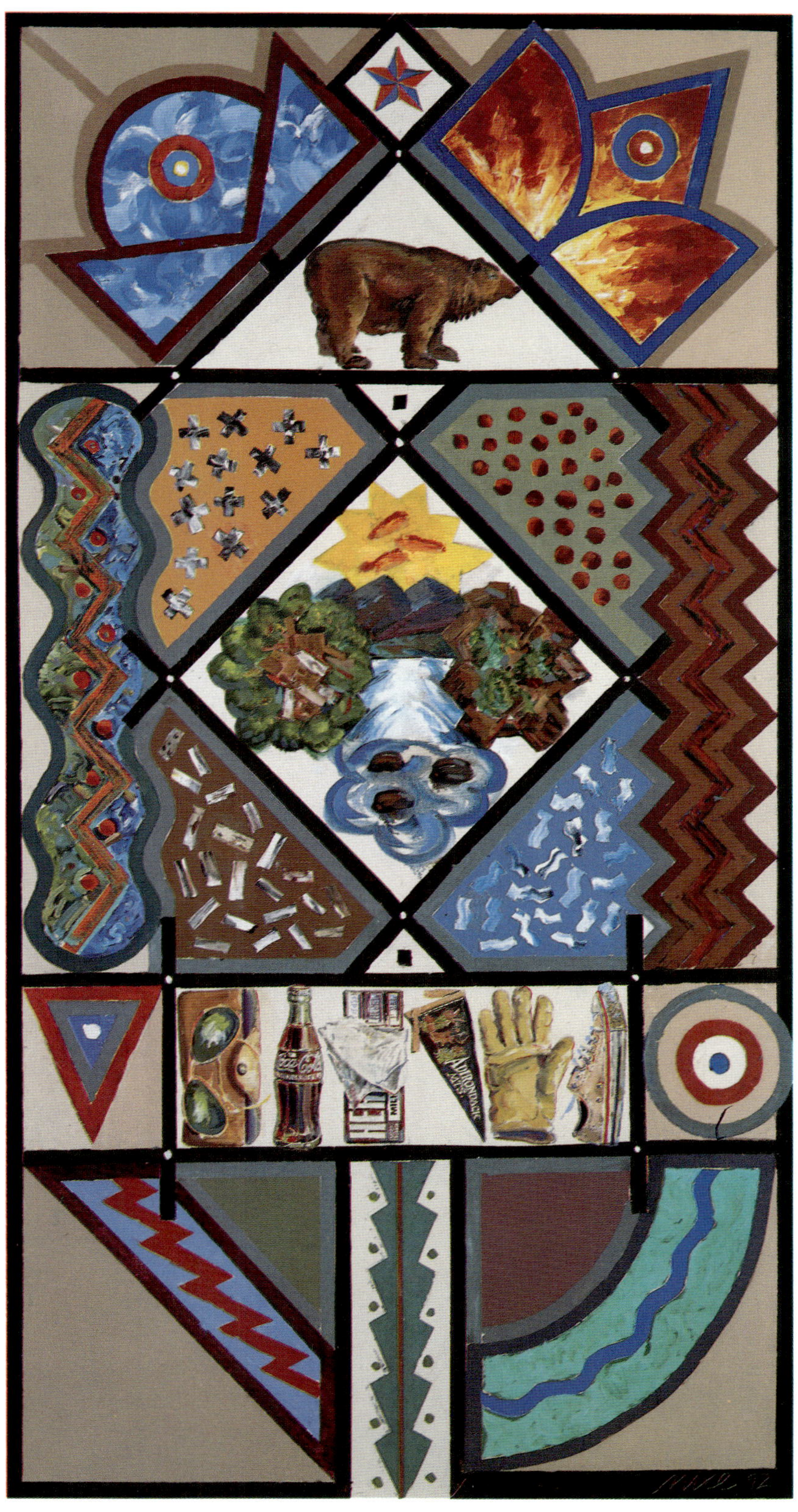

4

Positioned within a rectangle these artifacts of popular usage and consumption serve as a kind of *predella* (the small panel below the main altarpiece in Italian Renaissance paintings) for the artist's consciously totemic image. Commodified, like both nature and the painting itself, these commercial icons denote the world of human culture. Symbols of earth, fire, wind and water complete the design, providing formal appeal and iconographic coherence to the artist's vision.

In both honoring and consecrating the landscape, *Adirondack Totem* bodies forth ideas concerning the relationship of nature and the self that have engaged American artists since the early Romantic period. As the focus of the canvas, nature, perfect and divine, is privileged over humans and animals. Man, represented by his commodities, is afforded a marginal role, and distinctly perceived as "other." In acknowledging the dichotomy between the self and objectified nature, the artist starkly reformulates for modern viewers a long and sustained tradition of American landscape painting.[3]

Consciously discoursing with the art of the past, Nice's image reminds us that the Adirondacks have always been a charged landscape, a place where reality and the American imagination have intersected. The categories of experience inscribed within the painting, reverence for the sanctity of nature, the tenuous connections between man and the land, and the relationship of humans to animals have always provided the dominant subjects of the art of the Adirondacks.[4] Arguably, no region of America has persistently afforded artists a mental geography and cultural iconography of such variety and significance. Moreover, nowhere are mountains and valleys, sky and water, forests and fields as densely and dramatically juxtaposed. Finally the unrelenting confrontations between the public and private, history and futurity, God's creation and individual artistic creativity, have afforded the Adirondack north country an enduring place in the American mind. A locus of American exceptionalism, the northland has persistently stood for the nation as a whole.

Nature, however, did not initially enjoy absolute primacy over the affairs of men and women. The earliest high art incursions into the north woods were primarily encounters with history. Impelled by the desire to create a visual culture for the new nation, the first painters of the Hudson River School envisioned the Adirondacks as a stage for the pictorial re-enactment of a specifically American experience. Thomas Cole's several paintings based on James Fenimore Cooper's novel, *The Last of the Mohicans*, viewed the land as a site of colonial history, a landscape transformed by violence and regeneration.[5] His friend and contemporary Asher Durand's *Murder of Miss McCrea* (Fig. 2) projects the historic moment to the period of the Revolutionary War. Beneath the outspread branches of a large pine tree, savage Indians, allies of the British, attack a hapless female victim. The martyred fiancée of an English officer in Burgoyne's army, Jane McCrea (together with the resultant legend) served early America as a means of exploring the conflict between nature and culture, good and evil, democracy and monarchy.[6] The gloomy Adirondack forest setting (near Fort Edward) affords both a lurid backdrop to, and a natural adumbration of, the violent figural action.

The added knowledge that Durand's "history painting" was destined as a gift for a well-known French actor indicates that he, like Cole before him, was actively constructing a pictorial history for America, one that could bolster national self-confidence or, alternatively, persuade Europeans of the "significance" of American nature.

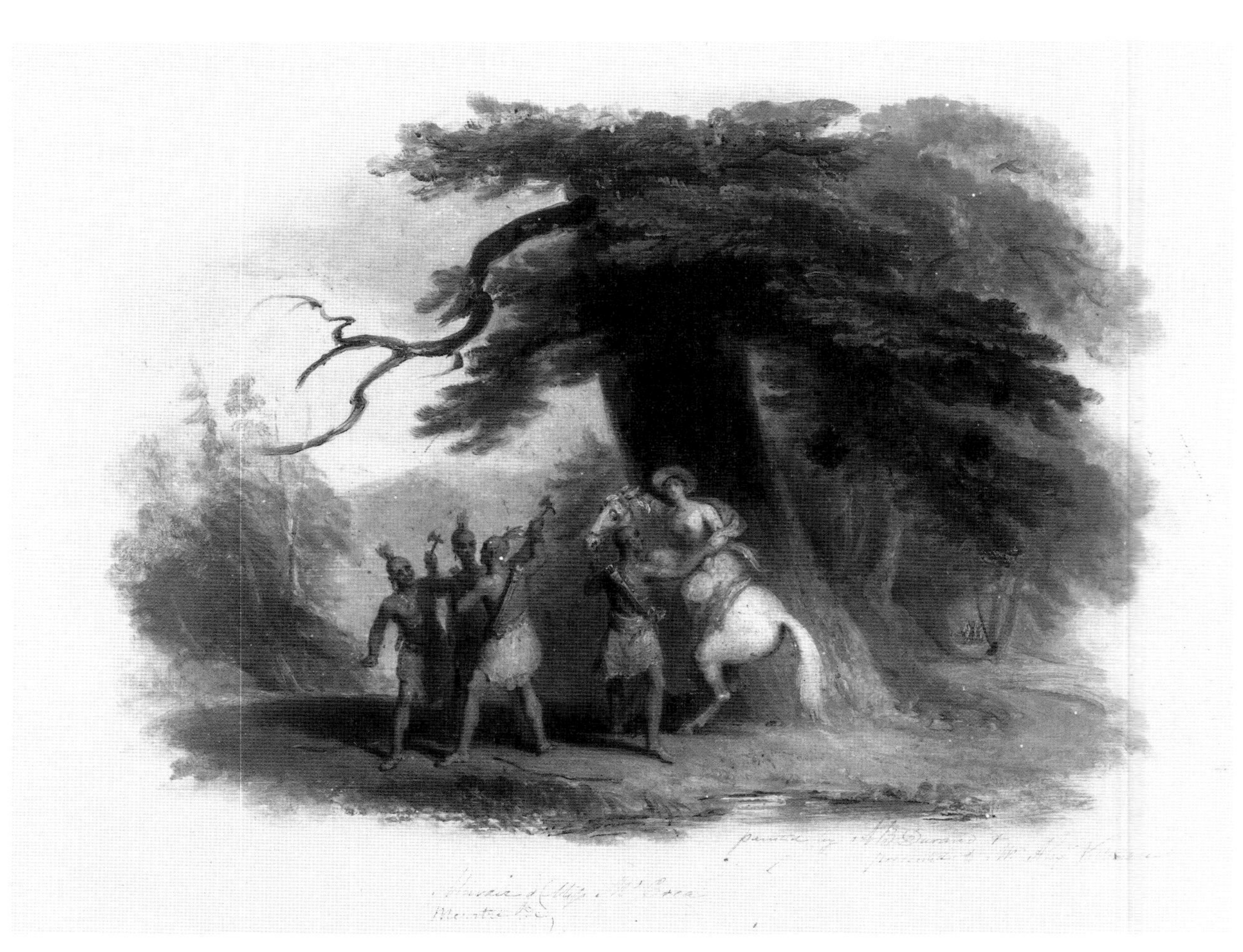

Additionally, Durand's view of nature as a setting for spectacle conferred the status of theater upon the wilderness, a conceit that would not have been lost on the Frenchman. Drawing upon resonant historic and patriotic themes of the Colonial and Revolutionary past, the Hudson River School painters discovered in the Adirondacks both a *theatrum mundi* and a landscape of "poetical associations," which could, in turn, be invested with a transfiguring freight of meaning. In these early 19th century narratives the avid Romantic appetite for dramatic "Association" was satisfied by an American landscape painted and written into aesthetic and cultural respectability.[7]

Another early 19th century strategy for conferring higher meaning upon the land was by invoking the aesthetic vocabulary of the European cult of the "sublime."[8] Charles Ingham's *The Great Adirondack Pass* of 1837 (Fig. 3), painted to document the first geological survey of the region, conforms with this well-known pictorial mode.[9] Small in relation to the vastness of nature and the evident traces of a powerful geology, the artist positions himself in a pose of rapt contemplation at the lower left of the canvas. Cyclopean glacial erratics, blasted stumps and strong contrasts of light and dark define a primordial wilderness in which man is an awe-struck observer and an intruder. The gigantic natural forms are contrasted with the tiny figure of the artist. Nature rather than man is the central protagonist in this pictorial drama. The Adirondack wilderness, in what is among the earliest instances, moves to center stage as human history is eclipsed by the vision of the primal landscape.

By positioning himself at the lower left of the composition in the act of sketch-

Fig. 2

ASHER B. DURAND

The Murder of

Miss McCrea

ca. 1839

Oil on board

12 1/2 x 17 5/8

Courtesy of

Fort Ticoderoga Museum

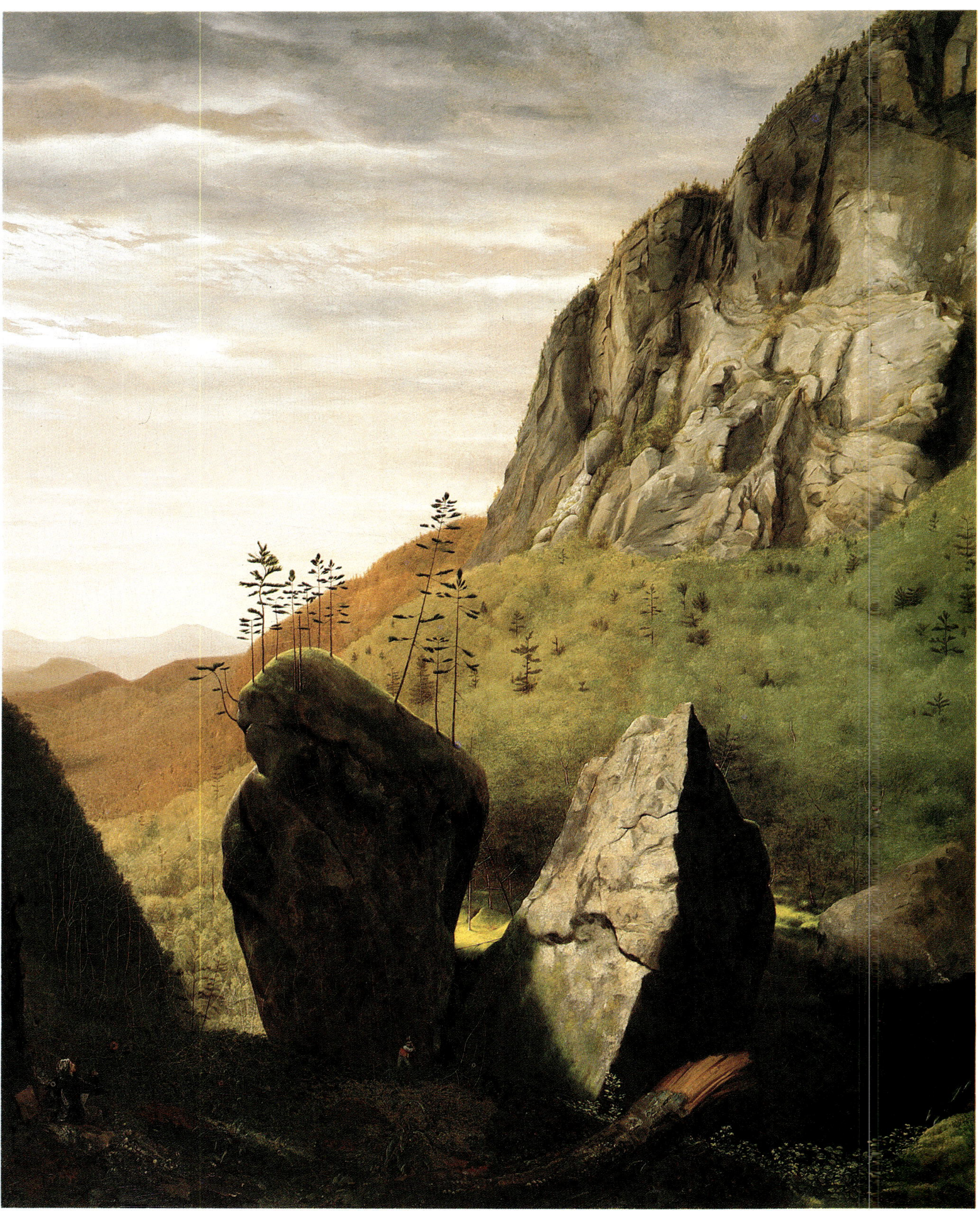

ing, the painter affirms the role of art in mediating the relationship with nature and structuring the perception of place for the popular imagination. The artist, in substituting an image for the land itself, performs an act of imaginative displacement that held considerable consequences for the future of the region. For most urbanites and armchair tourists, paintings, rather than the place itself, came to define reality. Better preserved on canvas than in fact, the wilderness emerged during the early 19th century as the iconic symbol of "nature's nation."

A later reprise of the Romantic fascination with geologic scale can be found in Samuel Colman's *AuSable River* (Checklist #5) of about 1869, where a small angler casting into a pool is contrasted with giant rough hewn rocks deposited by ancient forces. Here the insignificance of human enterprise is contrasted with the weighty traces of natural creation.

The year 1837 in which Ingham painted *The Great Adirondack Pass* also marks the naming of the Adirondacks by the New York State Natural History Survey.[10] In addition, this seminal year coincided with a celebrated visit to the region by the founding fathers of American landscape painting, Thomas Cole and Asher Durand.[11] Indeed, prior to 1837, there was no such place as the Adirondacks. For all intents and purposes they were "invented" by the State Natural History Survey and the pioneering landscapes of the early Hudson River School painters. This unpremeditated confluence of science and art served both to define the region and to introduce a unique regional identity into the national consciousness. Henceforth the Adirondacks were the largest and most accessible wilderness to the metropolitan East and, as such, contributed to the definition of our national character and destiny.

Fig. 3

CHARLES CROMWELL

INGHAM

The Great

Adirondack Pass, Painted

on the Spot

1837

Oil on canvas

48 x 40

Adirondack Museum,

Gift of Mr. and Mrs.

Harold Grout

For Ingham and his contemporaries the Adirondack Pass, also known as Indian Pass, evoked emotions of fear and exaltation. The geologist Ebenezer Emmons, in viewing the site, claimed that "it is from facts like these that we learn what mighty forces operated in former times."[12] Somewhat later (and from the perspective of a mammoth plate camera) the photographer Seneca Ray Stoddard viewed the identical landscape as "a grand old mountain ruin," providing a natural analogue to the castles of Europe.[13] For the Romantic traveler Joel Headley, it "was the most remarkable gorge in the country, if not the whole world," suggesting the "mysterious" and the "awful."[14] Finally, the painter Jervis McEntee found the Pass in 1851 to be "one of those wild scenes so full of majesty and sublimity which the Creator has found for us to look upon that we may better comprehend his boundless power."[15] Responding to the Adirondack Pass more as a sacred place than as a landscape of adversity, McEntee spoke for many an early visitor to the region.

The painter-poet Thomas Cole described his initiation to the north country in a short poem entitled *The Wild:*

> Friends of my heart, lovers of nature's works,
> Let me transport you to those wild, blue mountains
> That rear their summits near the Hudson's wave;
> Though not the loftiest that begirt the land,
> They yet sublimely rise, on their heights
> Your soul may have a sweet foretaste of heaven....

Written in 1826, Cole's verses equate the mountain wilderness with the Garden of Paradise, a conceit that would inform several of his paintings.[16]

anford Gifford's *A Twilight in the Adirondacks* (Fig. 4) articulates this perception of a spiritual landscape in pictorial form. Painted during the Civil War, the artist's austere and reductive vision of earth, sky and water is transfixed by a veil of blazing atmosphere. Representing the four elements as well as the presence of God in the landscape, Gifford's resplendent canvas invites comparisons with Emerson's Transcendentalism and the verses of the Fireside poets.[17] In such Luminist works as Gifford's *Twilight,* an aura of peace and tranquility is posited as a counterpoise to the strife of the political and military confrontation between North and South. Denoting God's Country, the northland is also made to bespeak the Union and American futurity.

As in earlier Adirondack landscapes, nature here looms over the activities of man. Campers, located on the shore of a large body of water, stand before the spectacle of nature representing itself in a flaming sea of color. A large glacial boulder, deposited on the shore of the lake, denotes the geological past and serves as a kind of wilderness pulpit for nature's votaries.

harles Heyde's nearly contemporaneous *Shelburne Point at Sunset* (Checklist #12) depicts the Transcendental vision of nature through a form of internal pictorial dialogue. Viewing the chain of the Adirondack Mountains together with a blazing sunset from the Vermont shore of Lake Champlain, Heyde contrasts a stump-filled foreground with the prospect of distant mountain glory. The juxtaposition of the pastoral foreground (replete with grazing cows) with the sublimities of the mountains carries with it an implied priority of wilderness over cultivated landscape. The passage from the mundane to the "higher

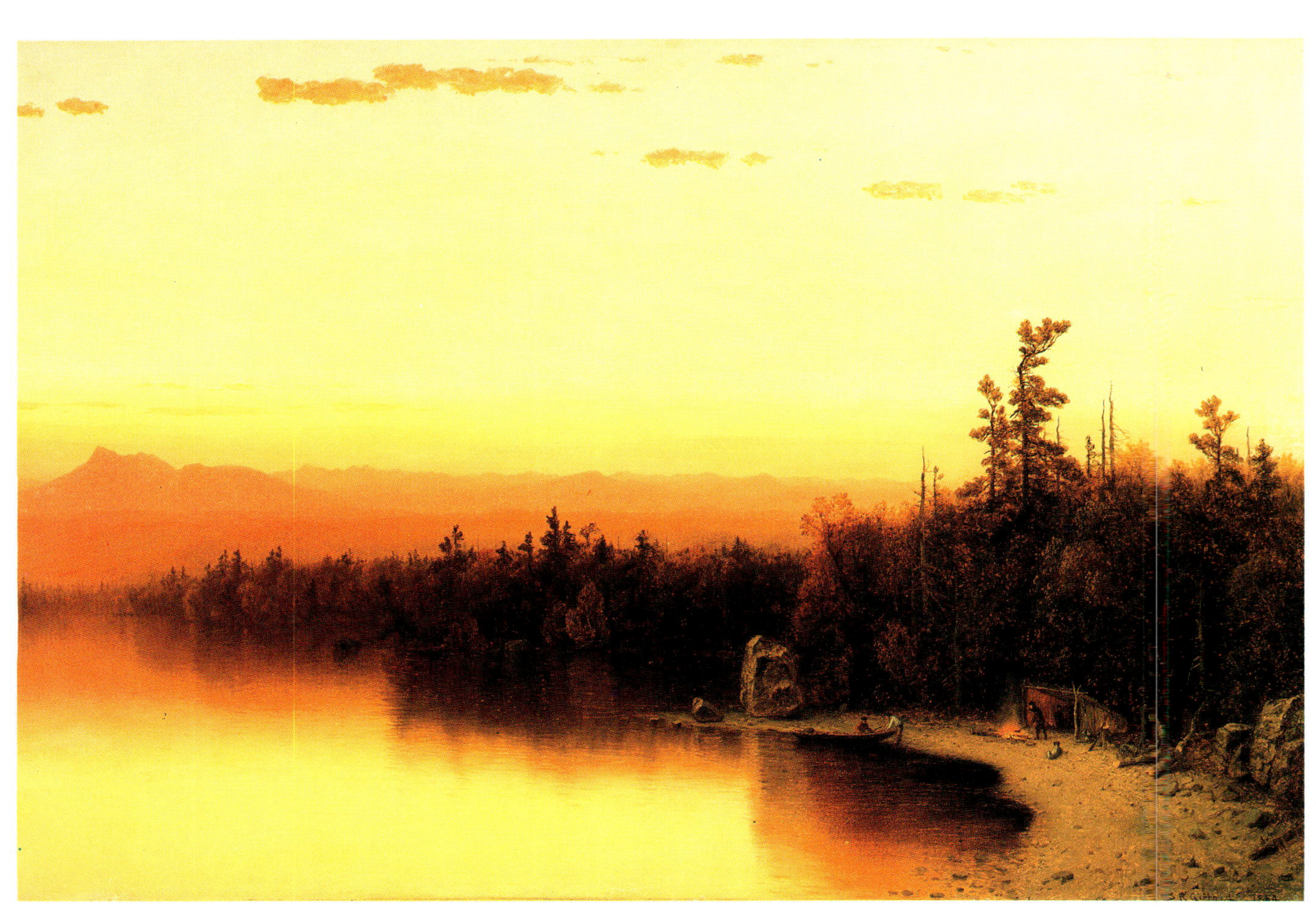

landscape" is mediated by the mirror-still body of water, the Transcendental "eye of heaven." A verbal equivalent to Heyde's theatrical vision is provided by Walt Whitman, the artist's brother-in-law, who, when viewing the actual scene on the shore of Lake Champlain, declared it to be "the finest show he had ever witnessed."[18]

For other mid-century enthusiasts of the Adirondacks the simple "facts" of nature were also as evocative of the divine as the more poetic confections of the early Romantics. William James Stillman's *Saranac Lake, Adirondack Mountains* (Fig. 5), for example, possesses the raw look of "unselective naturalism" advocated by English critic John Ruskin.[19] Painted at least partially out-of-doors, Stillman's meticulously detailed image of trees, water and sky appears almost photographic in its insistence upon the observed fact rather than the artifices of the studio. At the same time, the artist's obsessive realism was understood to function as a material metaphor for a higher spiritual reality. As numerous Romantic pantheists avowed in both paint and print, the immediate facts of nature are merely reflections of metaphysical truths. A member of the American Pre-Raphaelite Brotherhood (The Association for the Advancement of Truth in Art), Stillman believed as fervently as any American Congregational minister of the period that there are "tongues in trees and sermons in stone."[20]

The expedient medium of watercolor especially permitted painters of Adirondack "truth" to work directly in front of nature, recording the rock forms, trees and weather in a precise and analytical manner. James David Smillie's *Top of Giant's Leap*,

Fig. 4

SANFORD ROBINSON

GIFFORD

A Twilight in the

Adirondacks

1864

Oil on canvas

24 x 26

Adirondack Museum

14

Adirondacks (Checklist #36), painted on the morning of October 1, 1869, between 9 and 12:30 ("when I cooked my lunch"), is characteristic of the carefully detailed draftsmanship of the American Pre-Raphaelites. The painter's precise and elaborately finished technique contrasts strongly with the sketchy and expressive washes of later Adirondack watercolorists such as Winslow Homer, George Luks and John Marin (Checklist #'s 13, 22, 23).

Not all 19th century visitors to the Adirondacks, however, understood the landscape to be the book of nature and a repository of divine wisdom. The painter Eliphalet Terry (best known as the first teacher of Winslow Homer) viewed the homestead of the Baker family (Fig. 6), situated in the heart of the Adirondack wilderness, as a site for struggle, subsistence and survival. The log house, rail fences and conspicuous man-made stumps in the foreground of the picture indicate that humans also have a place, albeit a precarious one, in the wilderness. Less a reflection upon the pioneering past than a document of contemporary efforts to carve a life out of the north woods, Terry's painting possesses no visible overtones of transcendence. Rather the artist's stark palette and unidealized composition effectively suggests the harsh realities of life in the north woods.

Along similar lines, Homer Dodge Martin's depiction of *Iron Mine, Port Henry, New York* (Checklist #25) runs counter to the general image of the Adirondacks as an innocent and uncorrupted wilderness. Commissioned by the owner of the Bay

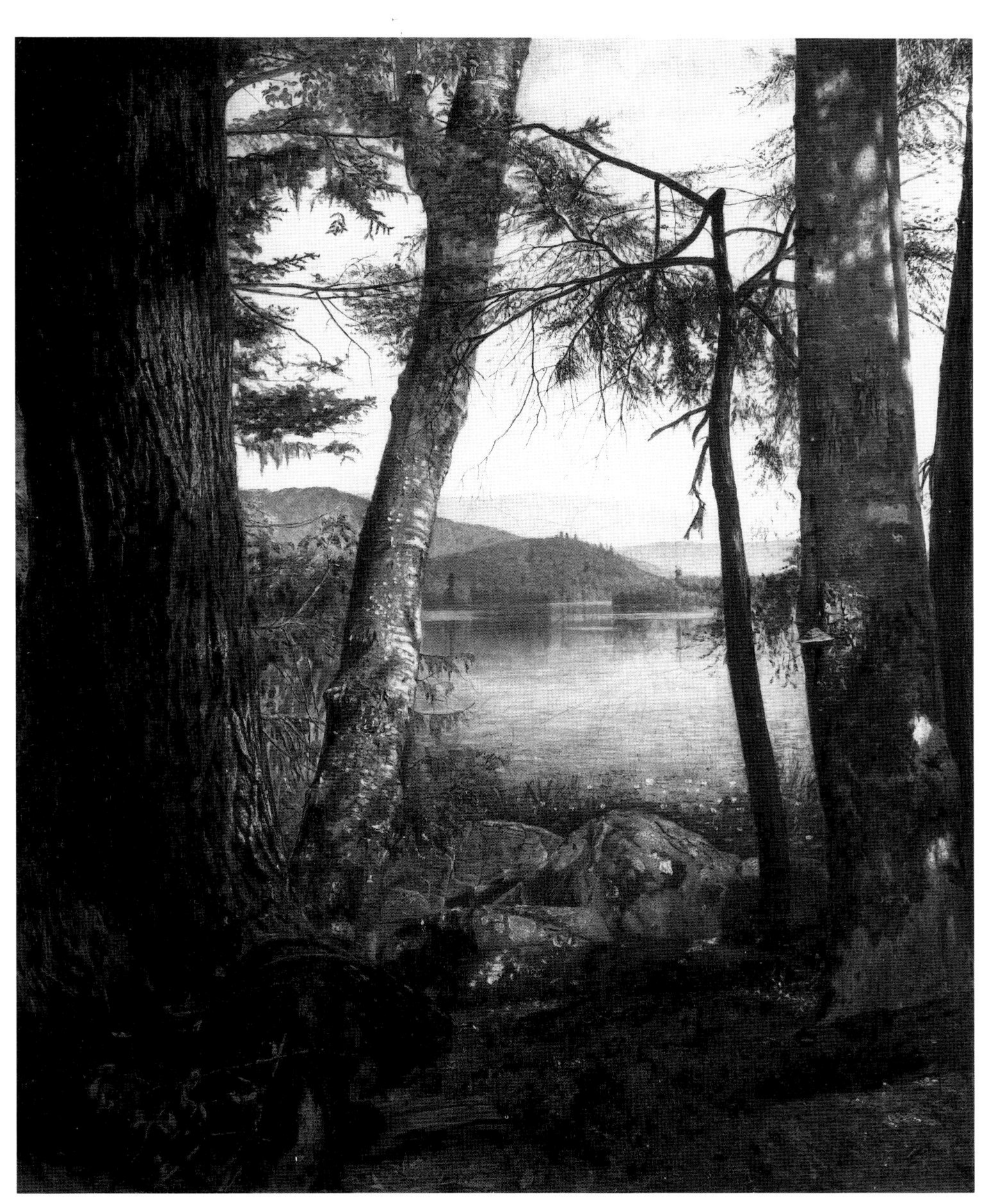

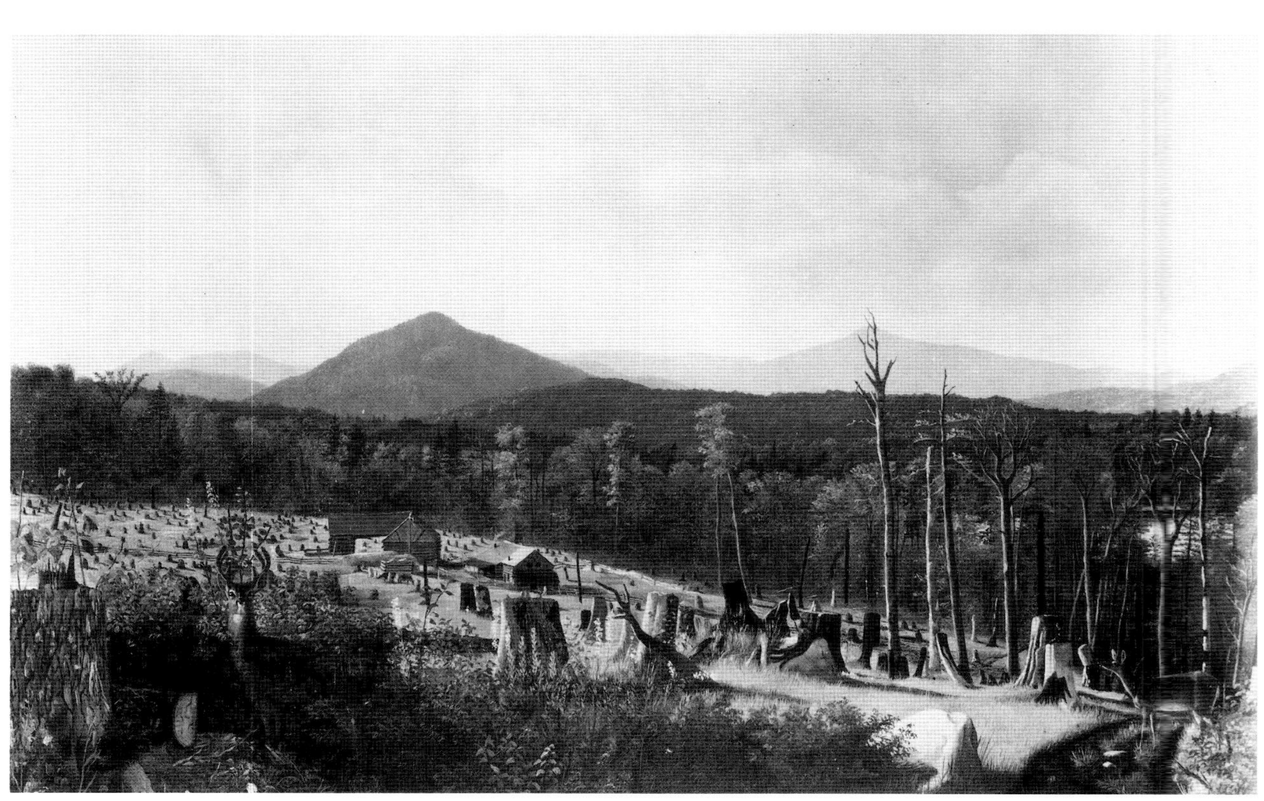

State Iron Mine Company, Martin's utilitarian "landscape" documents the technology of the extraction of ore from the iron rich region around Lake Champlain. Unencumbered by the studio conventions of Hudson River School painting, the artist's laconic image is composed of flat, horizontal planes rather than devoted to a deep recessional vista. Browns and greys, in lieu of the flaming vermilions and deep blues of his contemporaries, dominate this scene of enterprise. The absence of workers, blast furnaces and the active procedures of extraction indicate, however, that Martin sought to idealize mining by making it appear "natural" and non-intrusive.

I n 1869 the Reverend William H. H. Murray, a Congregational minister from Boston, published his *Adventures in the Wilderness: Or Camp Life in the Adirondacks.* Probably the most influential book ever written about the region, Murray's *Adventures* attracted throngs of tourists and sportsmen to the forests and lakes of the region in search of health and adventure. While the impact of the writer's "recreational revolution" has probably been overstated, landscape tourism accelerated dramatically after the Civil War.[21] Less concerned with spirituality and aesthetics than with adventure and recreation, Murray both shaped and reflected the rising popular perception of the Adirondacks as a vacationland. Alfred Thompson Bricher's *Boating Party on Lake George* (Fig. 7) is characteristic of numerous tourist paintings executed at the time. Against a vast expanse of sky, water and land, fashionably clad urbanites enjoy a summer outing in a boat. Clear skies and effervescent waters provide the setting for this convivial social drama. Reduced to "scenery," nature no longer possesses the resonant force of the sublime. As one contemporary writer in the *New York Times* observed: "The desert has blossomed with

Eliphalet Terry

Baker's Farm

1859

Oil on canvas

19 x 30

Anonymous.

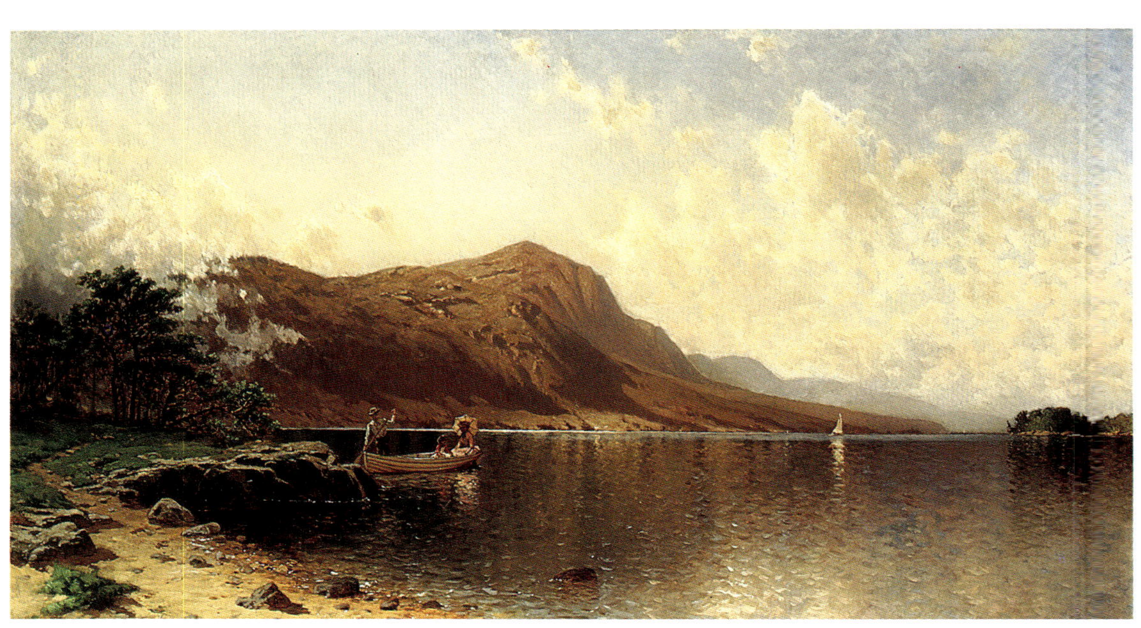

parasols and the waste places are filled with picnic parties, reveling in lemonade and sardines."[22]

Of similar intent such sporting scenes as Frederic Rondel's *A Hunting Party in the Woods* (Checklist #34) and Arthur Fitzwilliam Tait's *A Good Time Coming* (Fig. 8) also deploy the north woods as a locus for congenial human gatherings. Shunning the panoramic vistas favored by landscape painters, sporting artists focused on male comradeship set in the bosom of the deep forest. A social dialectic between city and country, sportsmen and guides, leisure and work, inform these paintings, which have more to do with the creature comforts of urbanites than with the virtues of pristine nature. Alternatively, Frederic Remington's *Spring Trout Fishing in the Adirondacks—An Odious Comparison of Weights* (Checklist #30) humorously envisions life in the woods from the vantage of a north country native. Unlike Rondel or Tait's "gentlemen," the artist's rustic woodsmen are concerned with their "catch" rather than the amenities of camp life. Intended to illustrate an article on fishing in *Harper's Weekly* of May, 1890, Remington's amiable narrative (like Murray's verbal sketches) helped establish the allure of the north country in the wider public consciousness.

A natural paradise for New Yorkers of the Gilded Age, the Adirondacks were often viewed as a vast, aristocratic game preserve. Indeed, in the eyes and minds of sportsmen, no other region of the eastern United States rivaled the north country for hunting and fishing during the second half of the 19th century. This status, however, was not without attendant problems. Tourism and hunting were often viewed as hostile activities. The same *New York Times* reporter pithily noted that "the piano has banished the deer from the entire region."[23]

Fig.7

....

ALFRED THOMPSON

BRICHER

Untitled: Boating Party

on Lake George

ca. 1867

Oil on canvas

26 x 48

Adirondack Museum

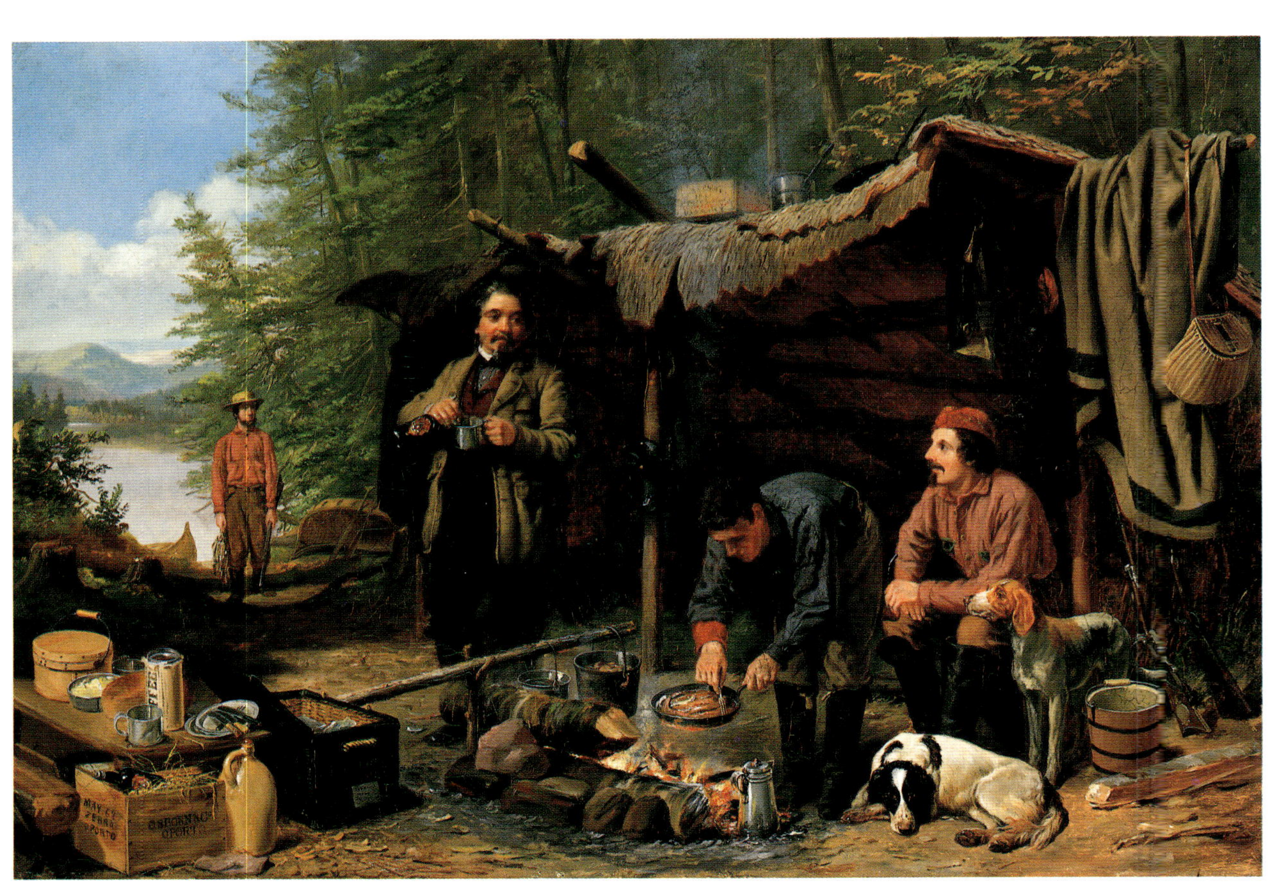

As Philip Terrie has demonstrated in his insightful study of the history of the
Adirondack Park, the immediate conflict between populist
tourists and elitist sportsmen during the Victorian era effectively
masked the larger threat to the region posed by logging.[24] As a
result, the jarring collision between the respective industries of
tourism, sport and logging did not surface until the last decade
of the 19th century when the environmental depredations of the
latter could no longer be ignored.

Few artists, moreover, before Winslow Homer chose
to comment pictorially on the role of logging in the
north woods. While Regis Gignoux's *Log Road in
Hamilton County* (Checklist #10) of 1844 repre-
sents an oblique reference to the practice of logging, and such
works as DeWitt Clinton Boutelle's 1867 view of *The Sacandaga River at Hadley, New York* (Checklist #2) includes a mill, a
dam and a sluice, most painters deliberately ignored the more
mundane aspects of life in the north woods. Even such artists as
Levi Wells Prentice, a native of New York's north country, pre-
ferred to envision the Adirondacks as an untrammeled wilderness, rather than a place where humans had already made sub-
stantial alterations in the landscape. Prentice's taut and linear
Smith's Lake, Adirondacks, N.Y. (Lake Lila) (Fig. 9) of 1883
allows no signs of human habitation to intrude upon his magis-
terial spectacle of wild nature.

Paintings such as *Smith's Lake* appear to have functioned ambivalently in their
popular reception. On the one hand the normative, Romantic
image of the Adirondacks as an unviolated wilderness no doubt
conveniently screened from many people the real threat to the
north woods posed by logging. On the other, Prentice's iconic
treatment of the land surely played a major role in stimulating a

22

Levi Wells Prentice
Smith's Lake,
Adirondacks, N.Y.
1883
Oil on canvas
26 x 48
Adirondack Museum,
Gift of Mr. and Mrs.
Harold K. Hochschild

reverence for nature that eventuated in the nearly contemporaneous legislation creating the Adirondack Park. While more utilitarian values of hunting, water-rights and health have also been cited as crucial determinants of this legislation, it cannot be denied that poets and painters were also responsible for creating a climate of opinion leading to the earlier creation of the Adirondack Forest Preserve. Aesthetics, in short, surely fostered the impulse to protect wilderness as much as political and social imperatives.

While the aesthetic and philosophical outlook that fostered the religious veneration of nature climaxed in the decades after the Civil War, a revolution from within the urban institutions of culture had begun to transform attitudes towards the Adirondack region as early as the 1870s. Homer Dodge Martin's *Lake Sanford* (Fig. 10), painted in 1870, dramatically challenges the older Romantic ideal of God-in-nature. A moody, crepuscular landscape, Martin's eroded and fire-ravaged world speaks more to the artist's personal vision than to the older public ideology of nature. No longer an icon of pantheistic worship, Martin's canvas is largely concerned with the processes of nature, and such biological principles as the procession from death and decay to regenerative new growth. Less committed to topography than to what is happening in the natural world, the artist does not recoil from the representation of mud, roots and dead trees. Nor does he balk at the description of clouds, wind and rain. Rather he documents the gritty "truths" of the natural process as opposed to the Romantic idealization of the wilderness. Grounded more in Darwin than the effusions of pantheistic clergymen, Martin's canvas rejects those scenic con-

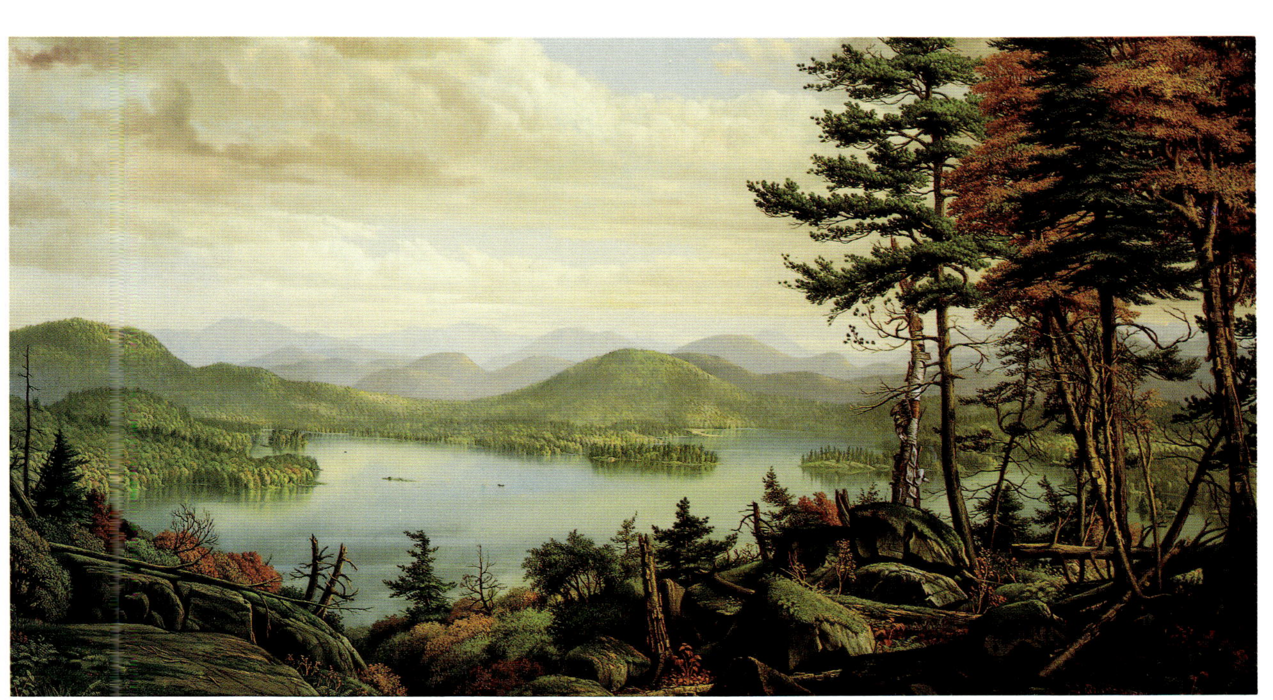

ventions by which nature is perennially viewed as clear, sunny and free of insects.

At the same time, *Lake Sanford* receives a regional inflection from the painter's brush that clearly distinguishes the Adirondack wilderness from the generic national landscape. The darkened palette and weight of atmosphere, together with the unusual admixture of dense woods, shimmering water and weather, provide an authentic "look" that can be associated with no other part of the country. For contemporary viewers, Martin's Adirondack landscapes spoke with a unique north country accent.

In addition, the artist's manner of painting differs strikingly from Hudson River School artists. Painted in the recollected tranquility of the studio, over charcoal sketches made on site, Martin's canvas is transitional from the tightly finished paintings of the early Romantic landscapists to the spontaneous mode of the later Impressionists. As such, *Lake Sanford* possesses a more "natural" and spontaneous look for a modern viewer than the precise and exacting work of the artist's contemporaries.

Due in large measure to the morbid coloration and the absence of compositional formulas, *Lake Sanford* also appears more internalized than earlier paintings of Adirondack "scenery." The brooding, tonalist palette of browns and greys, the lack of precise definition of natural forms, and the hazy atmospherics combine to promote an elegiac mood. The painter George Inness, another master of Tonalist mood, spoke for *Lake Sanford* when he claimed, "A work of art does not appeal to the intellect nor the moral sense. Its aim is not to instruct or edify but to awaken an emotion."[25]

In shifting the definition of reality from the object to the viewer, Martin anticipated more recent attitudes toward the representation of land-

Fig 10

HOMER DODGE MARTIN

Lake Sanford

1870

Oil on canvas

24 1/2 x 39 1/2

Courtesy of

The Century Association

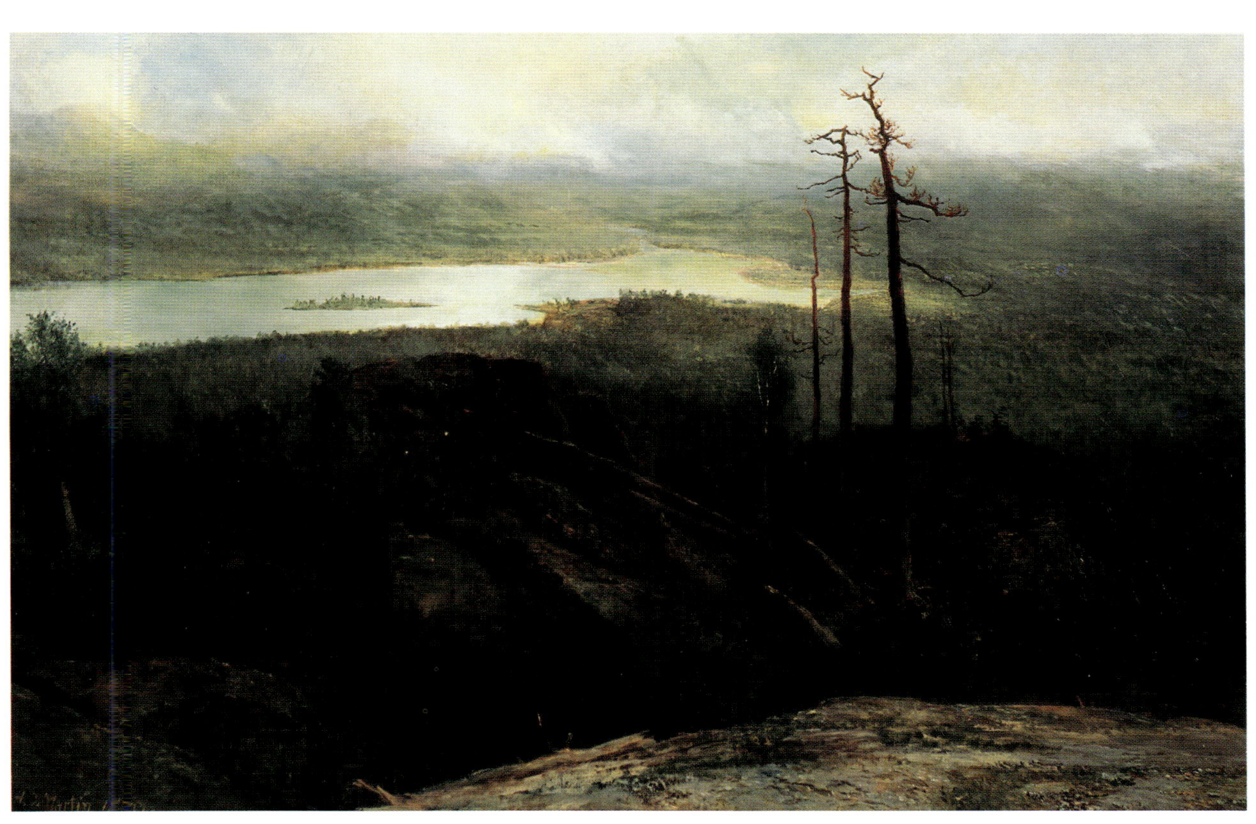

scape. His emotive and subjective approach contrasts markedly with the socially oriented attitudes of the earlier Hudson River School as Claudian formulas yield to private reflections and radically decentered compositions. Finally, paintings such as *Lake Sanford* also made new demands upon the consciousness of contemporary observers. Lacking the material certainties of earlier landscapes, Martin's canvas does not afford a definitive reading. Intimations of "Tonalist doubt" and "defeated hopes" commingle with older Romantic ideas concerning the role of nature. Ambiguously structured and psychologically complex, *Lake Sanford* is in all respects a paradigmatic object of the "Brown Decades."[26]

The implicit alienation of the artist from a realistically conceived external world evidenced by *Lake Sanford* lead to a crisis in painting that persists in the 20th century. In viewing art primarily as self-expression rather than representation, Martin contributed not only to the dismantling of the Romantic view of nature, but invented a radically new way of composing landscape. Assigning a rough equality to space, form and color, the artist depicts nature as a balance of elements rather than a sequence of hierarchies. Subsumed into the mood of the landscape, the artist's sensibility, rather than the phenomenal forms of nature, is the real subject of the painting. As an arrangement of color, tone, shape and atmosphere, *Lake Sanford*, above all, is a painting by Homer Dodge Martin before it is a depiction of a place. No doubt the increasing ability of photography to capture appearances also contributed at the time to the artist's aversion to topographic description.

Like many Adirondack paintings, however, *Lake Sanford* alludes to the elements of fire, earth, wind and water. Reifying nature's processes through the lens of his subjective vision, the painter perceived the north woods as an elemental landscape, a place where mind and matter are inextricably linked. Something akin to this attitude was articulated by a contemporary critic who observed that Martin's painting was "that duplex image in which external nature fused itself with him, who was also a part of nature."[27] In collapsing the traditional separation between nature and the self, the artist projected his psychological morbidity onto the land, which became, in turn, the mirror of his sensibility.

The greatest painter of the Adirondacks, Winslow Homer, was uniquely endowed both physically and aesthetically to penetrate the hidden core of the north country. An avid sportsman, he knew the mountains, lakes and forests of the region better than any artist before and possibly since his time. His brilliant watercolors of fishing and hunting are the most technically complex and physically immediate sporting images ever painted. Often executed from the vantage of a solitary angler or hunter, these on-site sketches possess unrivaled directness in the description of both place and action. *Casting, "A Rise"* (Checklist #13), a late watercolor, captures the moment when a flycaster arrests his line in full flight in order to launch it forward. The focused concentration of the angler, combined with the stillness of the deep forest, creates a unified occasion without precedent in the art of the Adirondacks. Broad washes of opaque and transparent color define the material and psychological continuum between man and nature.

The bright palette and active brushwork of American Impressionism found little space for expression in the turn-of-the-century penumbra of the north country. The difficulties of travel in the region, in combination with the obligation to paint *en-plein-air*, discouraged artists from venturing far into the Adirondack wilderness. The bite of the ubiquitous and dreaded black fly (apparently more feared by Impressionists than by Pre-Raphaelites) no doubt also served as a deterrent to extended sketching out of doors. More importantly, the cultural erosion of the ideal of wilderness (Ruskin's "failure of nature") also contributed to the relative disinterest in the region by painters in search of light and leisure.[28] In this regard the suburb, the home, the garden displaced the deep woods as the site of modern sensibility. Moreover, pastoralism (the celebration of the domesticated landscape) began to emerge as the dominant view of American nature during the period and to a large degree deflected artistic interest away from the Adirondacks.

A small watercolor (Checklist #11) by Childe Hassam, documenting a Lake George camping trip with his friend and colleague Frederic Remington, is one of the few works from the period executed in the Impressionist manner. Deceptively simple, Hassam's vibrantly colored sketch contrasts strongly with the weighty artistic conceptions of earlier generations. A slightly later watercolor by George Luks entitled *Mountain Stream* (Checklist #22) also appears to be an on-site *memento* of an agreeable Adirondack vacation. No aura of transcendence informs these delightful watercolors as the active visible brushstrokes of the artists denote a shift from divine to human creation.

The large oil paintings of Gustave Wiegand, executed while he lived four to five months of the year at the Adirondack hamlet of Blue Mountain Lake, provide an exception to the general aversion of Impressionists to the region. Wiegand's *Blue Mountain* of 1914 (Fig. 11) is one of the rare winter scenes (Jonas Lie's view of the stable at Kamp Kill Kare near Raquette Lake, Checklist #21, is another) painted in the north country. No doubt the absence of leaves from the trees together with the presence of bright snow and blue sky rendered Wiegand's canvas amenable to the blandishments of the Impressionist aesthetic.

Two towering personalities dominate the artistic perception of the Adirondacks during the early and middle decades of the 20th century, the periods of early and high Modernism. The first, the photographer Alfred Stieglitz, was instrumental in introducing several of the first generation of early American Modernists, such as Georgia O'Keeffe and John Marin, to the Adirondacks. The second, the sculptor David Smith, both through his art and his long term residency near Lake George, influenced at least two important Abstract Expressionist painters to envision both the land and the cultural landscape from the vantage of the New York School.

Stieglitz's numerous photographs of Lake George are among the earliest efforts in America to employ the medium for fine arts purposes. As has frequently been noted, his *Equivalents* are meant to be read both as topography and as abstract designs. In a like manner his wife Georgia O'Keeffe viewed the landscape around Lake George as a locus for formal and representational experimentation. Characteristically, however, O'Keeffe rejected her husband's more spatial and atmospheric vision. Her decorative colors and planar forms generally aspire to a high degree of autonomy from the "real" world, a level of abstraction that was seldom ventured by the photographer.

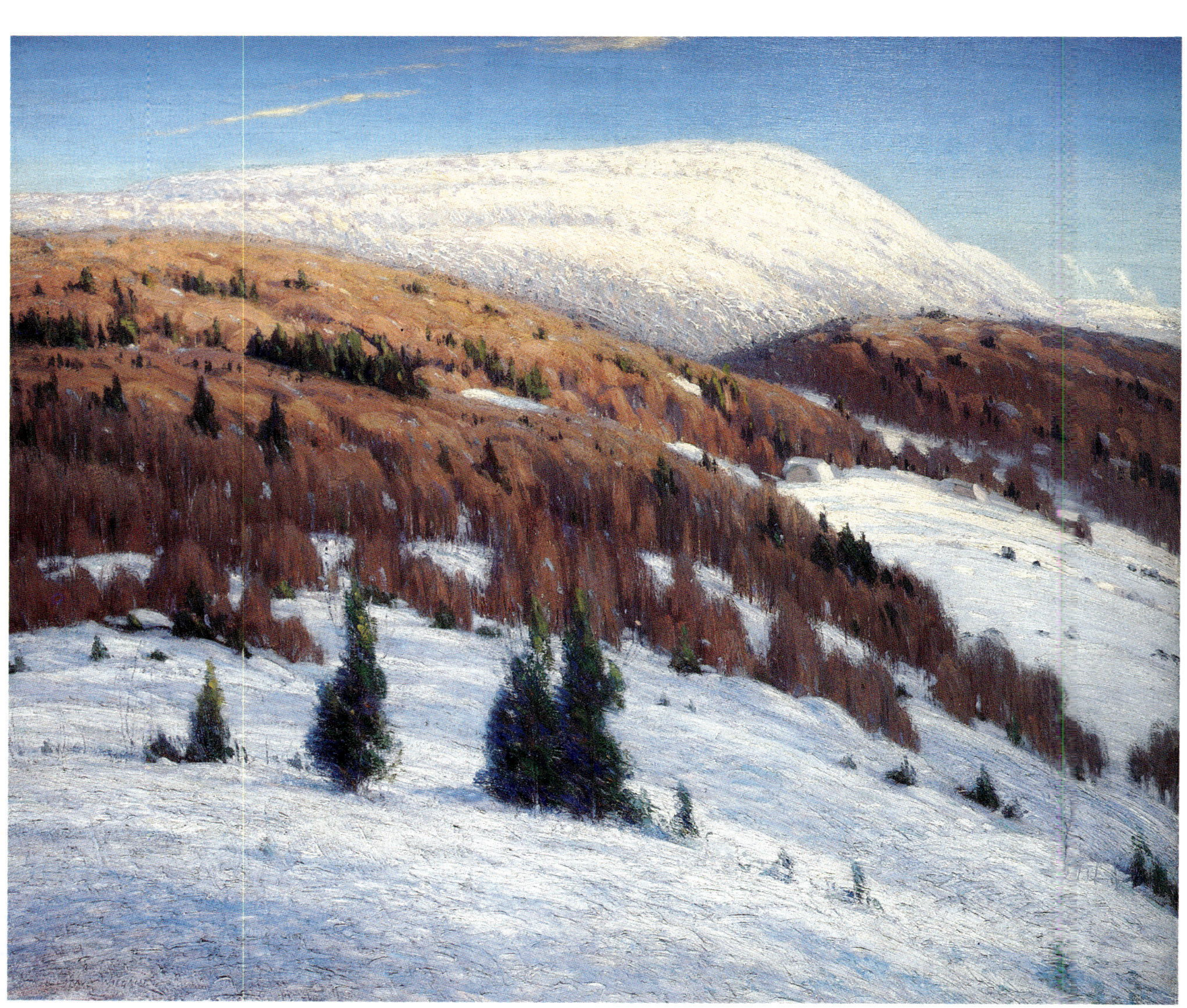

Maple and Cedar (Red) Lake George (Fig. 12) of 1923 is one of O'Keeffe's earliest Lake George tree "portraits" and is composed of swirling maple leaves and conical cedars outlined against a turbulent sky. The autumnal hues of red, green, and lavender are similar to those employed by Hudson River School painters almost a century before, but the magnified forms of trees and leaves are emphatically modern in their patterned, ornamental treatment. Exploiting the flatness of the canvas and the expressive nature of color, the artist reduced her painting to a strong, elemental design symbolizing the dual perfections of nature and art. For O'Keeffe, one of the first women ever to paint in the Adirondacks (for an interesting exception see Checklist #6), the religion of art effectively balanced the religion of nature.

John Marin's vibrant water color series of *Lake George* from 1928 can also be viewed as a form of homage to Stieglitz and his beloved vacation retreat. Painted during a visit to his mentor's summer home, they depict a landscape that had intrigued the painter since at least 1911. For Marin the Adirondack landscape appeared to be an active organism, living and breathing and with the mountains, "pushing and pulling" and "fighting and being fought against."[29] In a letter to Stieglitz, Marin wrote about the Lake George experience: "I am thinking of you and all that happened up there and the wonderful time I had. . . . Too I was made to feel by O'Keeffe and her sister that I wasn't exactly a nuisance. . . . It comes out in the end that those dogoned [*sic*] nature laws must be obeyed somehow or other."[30]

Like the painter Charles Ingham almost a century earlier, Marin viewed the Adirondack mountains as a repository of geological forces. In addition he thought of humans as intruders, as they seldom

Fig. 11

GUSTAVE ADOLF

WIEGAND

Blue Mountian

ca. 1914

Oil on canvas

41 x 48

Adirondack Museum,

Gift of

Mrs. Paul R. Tilson,

artist's daughter

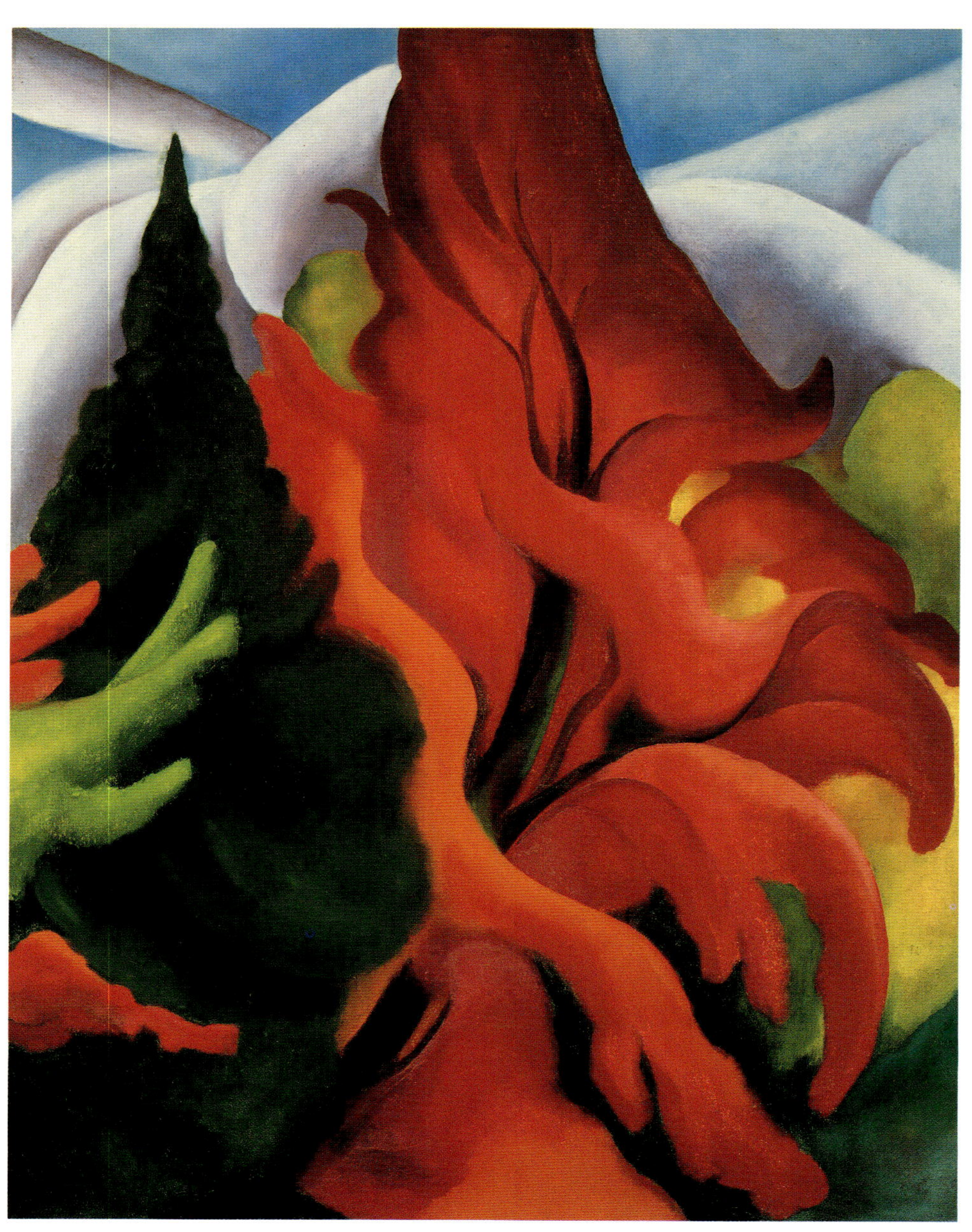

appear in his work. Commenting on his preference for nature, he once observed: "Mountains, streams and trees are so sympathetic. Damned if I find most humans so."[31]

Distilling his private sensation of the mountains, lakes, and forests into dynamically contrived compositions, the artist synthesized elements of Cubism, Futurism and Expressionism to achieve his powerful vision. For Marin, however, the organic vitality of nature was also a metaphoric projection of his own personal artistic struggle with the conflicting demands of abstraction and representation. In *Fulton Chain, Adirondacks, No.2* (Fig. 13) of 1912 Marin tilts the landscape and forces its forms to cohere within the frame of the image. Creating a pictorial surrogate for nature rather than a visual record, Marin enlivened his painting with light, transparent washes of color to create against the whiteness of the paper a scintillating surface pattern. His watercolors, to be sure, take as a point of departure the artist's perception of the natural world, but more importantly they are highly self-conscious aesthetic constructs. Additionally, they document the artist's visceral engagement with the Adirondacks as well as his choice of wilderness as a retreat from the stress of modern urban life.

Somewhat analogously, Harold Weston's numerous Adirondack oil paintings of the 1920s and 30s are the product of a long and impassioned relationship with the land. Fusing the decorative approach of O'Keeffe with the dynamic painterly manner of Marin, Weston created a body of work that is reflective of his elemental vision of the landscape, as well as a quasi-autobiographic account of his life in the Adirondacks. Like many of the early moderns, Weston was a student of New England Transcendentalism and Theosophy. Investing his canvases with the intensity of his

GEORGIA O'KEEFFE
Maple and Cedar (Red)
Lake George
1923
Oil on canvas
25 x 20
Collection of Mr. and
Mrs. Gerald P. Peters,
Santa Fe, New Mexico

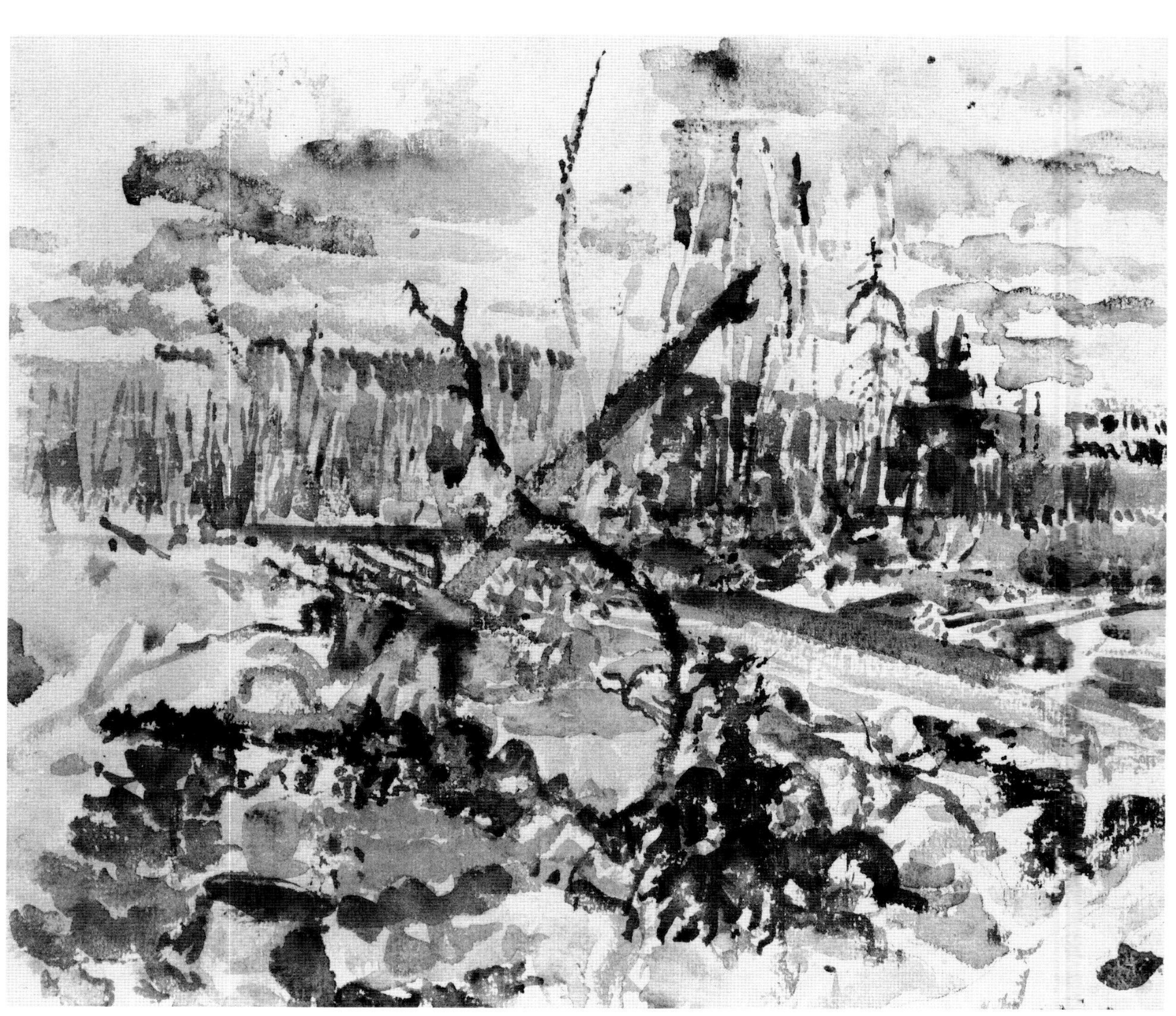

emotional response to the mountains, sky and water, the painter created a highly personal landscape image suffused with energy and vitality.[32]

While such paintings as *Birch Tree* (Checklist #42) reflect strategies of isolation and magnification derived from O'Keeffe, panoramic vistas like *Clouds—Upper Ausable Lake* (Checklist #43) reveal in their dynamic brush work and strident coloration an expressive treatment of landscape similar to Marin's. Extending the tradition of representing the Adirondacks as wilderness into the early 20th century, Weston further allied many of his compositions with the scenic panoramas of high Romanticism.

An antithetical point of view resides in the numerous pastoral landscapes of Rockwell Kent painted from the mid-1920s throughout the north country and later at Asgaard, his Adirondack farm near AuSable Forks. As the ascendant vision of nature, the pastoral displaced wilderness increasingly during the early 20th century. Like the Expressionists Marin and Weston, Kent envisioned the Adirondacks as a place of retreat from modern society and a safe refuge for myth. Conversely, such works as *At Peace* (Fig. 14) embody anti-modern impulses, both stylistically and ideationally. A field of dreams rather than a site of modernist energies, the Adirondacks are embedded in the amber of the artist's nostalgic vision of pastoral refuge.[33] Formally, Kent's austere realism reflects the simplicity of much early American painting, as does the conventional structure of his compositions. Like many of his "Regionalist" contemporaries, the artist intended his hard-edged rural style to counter the painterly mode of the urban *avant-garde*. Viewing the mountains as "symbols of immutability" rather than deposits of force,

Fig. 13

JOHN MARIN
Fulton Chain,
Adirondacks, No. 2
1912
Watercolor on paper
13 3/4 x 16 1/4
Adirondack Museum

the artist developed a taut landscape style that further recalls the primitive reductions of 19th century folk art.[34]

36

The W.P.A. painter Amy Jones' triptych of the St. Regis Reservation (Fig. 15) depicts the mundane activities of native Americans in the north country during the 1930s. Displacing the "natural behavior" of Indians with the industry of the white man, the artist subverts the traditional role assigned them by Romantic painters. Her monumental, linear style is enlisted in the representation of a quasi-religious and semi-utopian vision of tribal life in which salvation is attained through the dignity of labor. Her vibrant repertorial watercolors of skating and skiing in 1937 at Saranac Lake (Checklist #'s 16 & 17) depict the modern vogue for winter sports. In focusing international attention on the north country, the Olympic Winter Games at Lake Placid in 1932 and 1980 are connected with one of the most important aspects of the future of the Adirondacks.

Fig. 14

....

ROCKWELL KENT

At Peace

1940

Oil on canvas

28 x 40

Courtesy of D. Wigmore

Fine Art, Inc., New York,

New York

The eccentric modernist Florine Stettheimer revises yet another feature of the 19th century Adirondack pictorial canon. *Lake Placid* of 1919 (Checklist #37), a form of scenic conversation piece with connections to Victorian tourist views as well as the rococo idylls of Watteau, celebrates the world of her family and friends in a congenial setting of mountains and lakes.[35] Despite her friendship with Stieglitz and O'Keeffe, the artist developed a personal, insouciant view of the region as a vacationland that relates as much to the tourist landscapes of the previous century as to the abstractions of the early moderns.

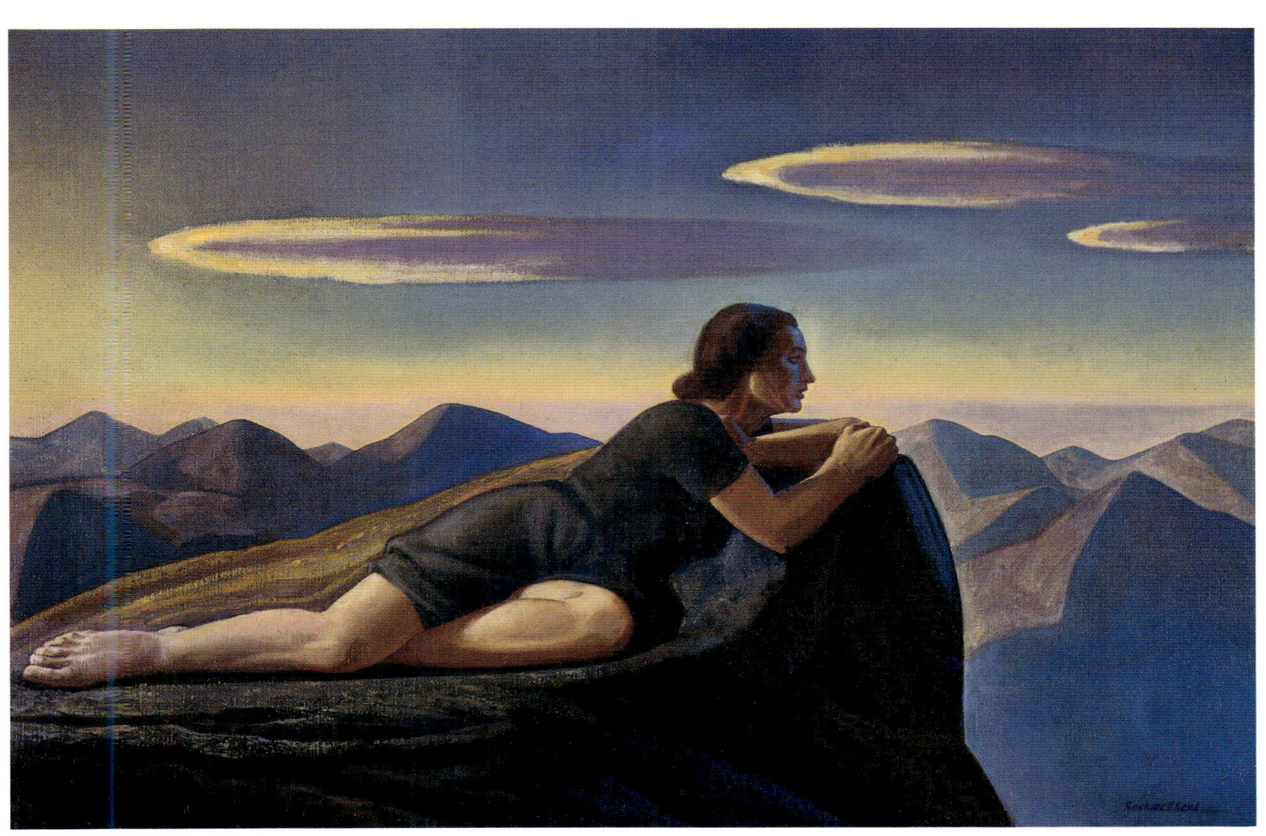

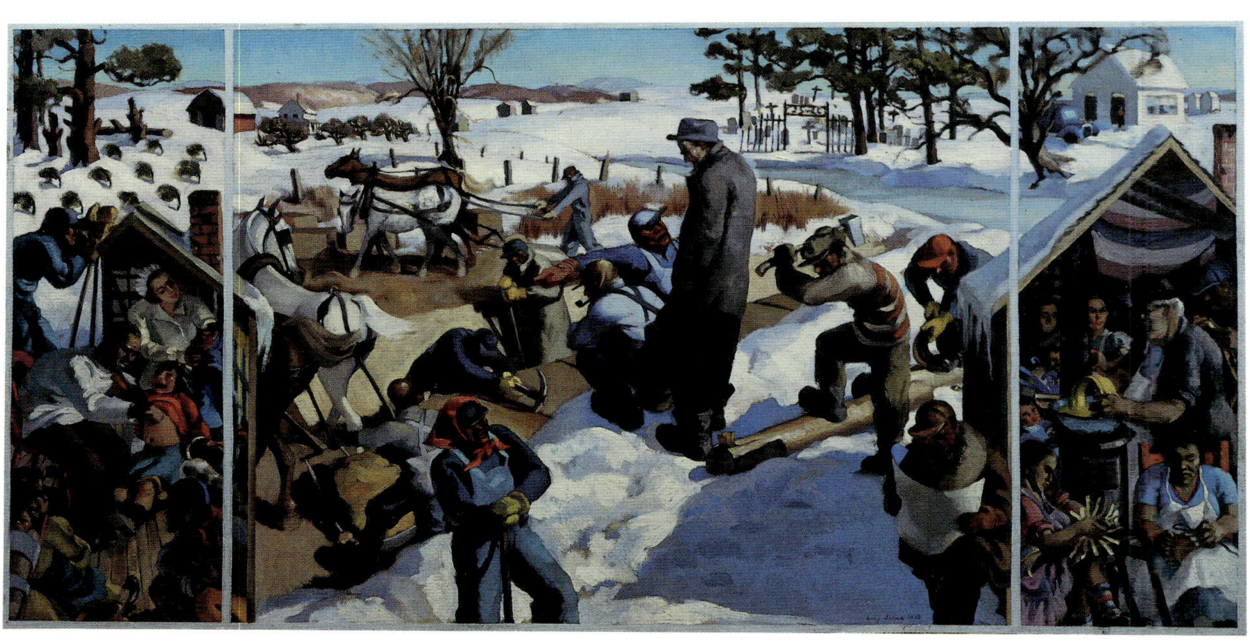

David Smith's studio at Bolton Landing on Lake George was the site of the master's most important sculptural works. Though he often referred obliquely to the landscape in his sculpture, Smith—like Stieglitz before him—was indirectly responsible for several important paintings of Adirondack subjects produced by friends and contemporaries. Ranging from Willem de Kooning's *Bolton Landing* of 1957,[36] an aggressively gestural Abstract Expressionist landscape (one of the artist's earliest), to Helen Frankenthaler's vibrant gouache of the same title (Checklist #8), painted in 1960, these works either directly respond to the experience of nature or, in the case of Frankenthaler, to Smith's sculpture.[37] Paradoxically, Helen Frankenthaler's pictorial celebration of Smith's art rather than the land itself belies the fact that she, of all the Abstract Expressionists, was the most actively engaged with the representation of "scenic remembrance pictures."[38]

Among prominent artists of the last few decades, there has emerged a number of interesting postmodern strategies for depicting the Adirondacks. Several of Allen Blagden's recent watercolors, for example, discourse energetically with the works of the Adirondacks' greatest painter, Winslow Homer. Exploring the nature of an image's connection to its source, *The Broad Axe* of the mid-1980s (Fig. 16), for example, addresses the question of an original work of art and the modern representation of it. Reminiscent of a well-known Homer watercolor entitled *The Woodcutter*, Blagden positions his woodsman at the juncture of the past and present.[39] His back turned to the spectator, Blagden's dominant and dominating figure surveys the landscape

Fig. 15

....

AMY WISHER JONES
St. Regis Reservation
1937
Oil on masonite
28 x 53
Adirondack Museum

from a rocky vantage. With the eyes of a tourist he gazes upon the wilderness while grasping the utilitarian axe of civilization. The incongruity of pose, together with the presence of the archaic axe, conjures up numerous unanswered, and ultimately unanswerable, questions about the meaning of the painting. The land, viewed from a privileged vantage, appears to be at once both spectacle and a locus of speculation.

A long-time summer resident at Saranac Lake, Blagden is, by his own admission, concerned with the widening gap between nature and culture. At the same time his tightly organized and minutely realistic watercolors are retrospective, seeking to capture, in the words of the artist, "the essence of many things remembered."[40] Though many of Blagden's watercolors depict humans engaged in fishing and hunting, *The Broad Axe* holds special resonance for anyone concerned with the future of the Adirondack Park and the conflicts between those who visit and those who live and work there.

Fig. 16

ALLEN BLAGDEN

The Broad Axe

ca. 1986

Watercolor on paper

40 x 25

Courtesy of Mongerson-Wunderlich Galleries, Chicago, Illinois

Don Wynn's *Campfire* of 1975 (Fig. 17) also alludes to a Homer painting of almost a century before.[41] Shifting the central protagonists from a group of men to a solitary woman, Wynn engages the informed viewer in a dialogue between the past and the present. Defining the wilderness experience from the vantage of a solitary woman rather than male comradeship, the artist creates a scene of reflection and introspection. His weary female camper, lost in a gentle melancholic reverie bordering on despondency, recalls the meditative mood established by Winslow Homer in several of his paintings of women in the mountains.[42] The use of a bold chiaroscuro light connects *Campfire* with the still older traditions of baroque painting. In yet another reference to pre-Romantic art, the artist's female

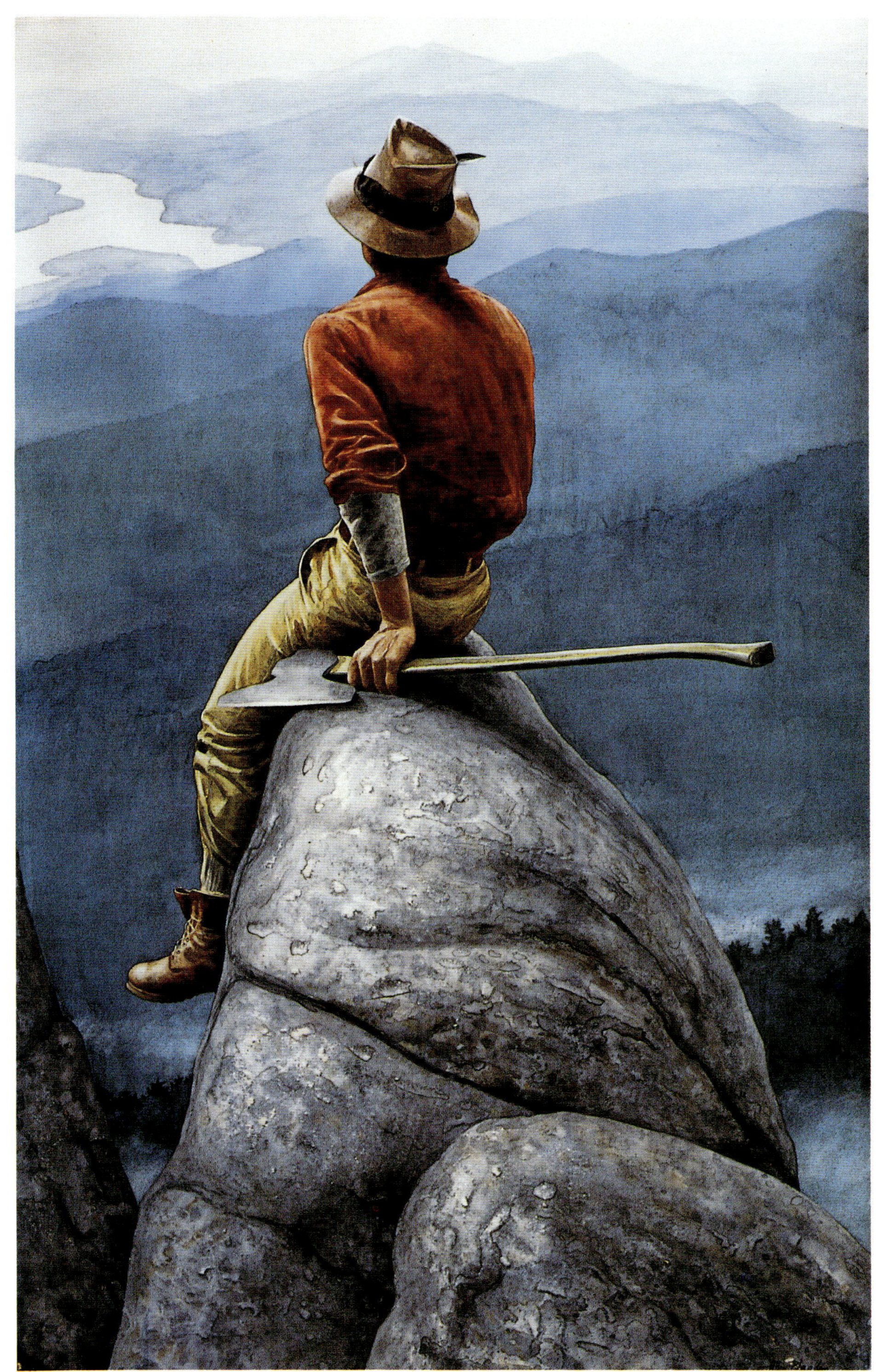

camper dominates the natural setting in a manner foreign to most American painting. This reversal of the usual relationship between humans and the Adirondacks suggests the current dilemma faced by anyone contemplating the future of the region. In setting aside such places as the Adirondack Park for wilderness recreation, Wynn intimates, we inadvertently run the risk of loving it to death. Like "Murray's Fools" over a century ago, the modern camper still confronts the dilemma posed by the contemplation of the ideal of a wilderness experience and its reality.

At another level the exhaustive catalogue of things required for modern camping recall the still-life inventory of artifacts found in the *predella* of Don Nice's *Adirondack Totem*. Where Wynn's socks, gloves, cans and cooking pot are major accessories of camplife, Nice's symbols possess a more unsettling relationship to his central image. Arriving at a similar place by different pictorial routes, Wynn and Nice meet halfway between two artistic worlds in representing modern man's alienation from the natural environment.

Frank Owen's monumental 8' x 24' *Floor of the Forest* (Fig. 18) addresses the traditional dichotomy between man and nature from a radically new perspective. Employing as his governing metaphor the layered detritus of the forest floor, Owen impresses branches, leaves, twigs and rocks into overlapping glazes of acrylic paint, leaving a fugitive impression of these natural shapes in the transparent matrix of the painting. Conjoined with these references are photographs of people made by the artist and embedded in the paint by a process of carbon transfer. Chaotic and non-hier-

Fig. 17

Don Wynn
Campfire
1975
Oil on canvas
90 x 72
Adirondack Museum,
Gift of Mr. and Mrs. J.
Richardson Dilworth

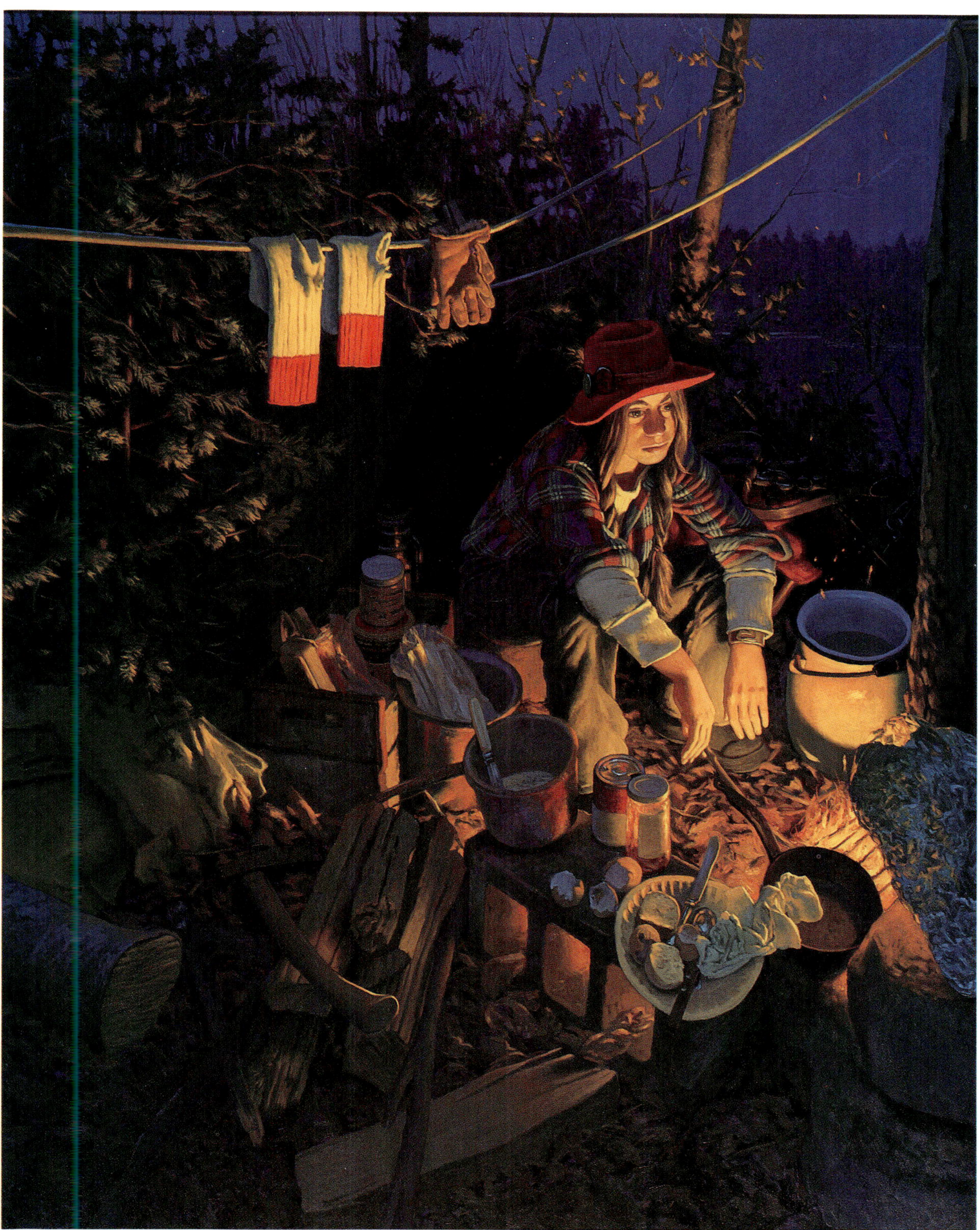

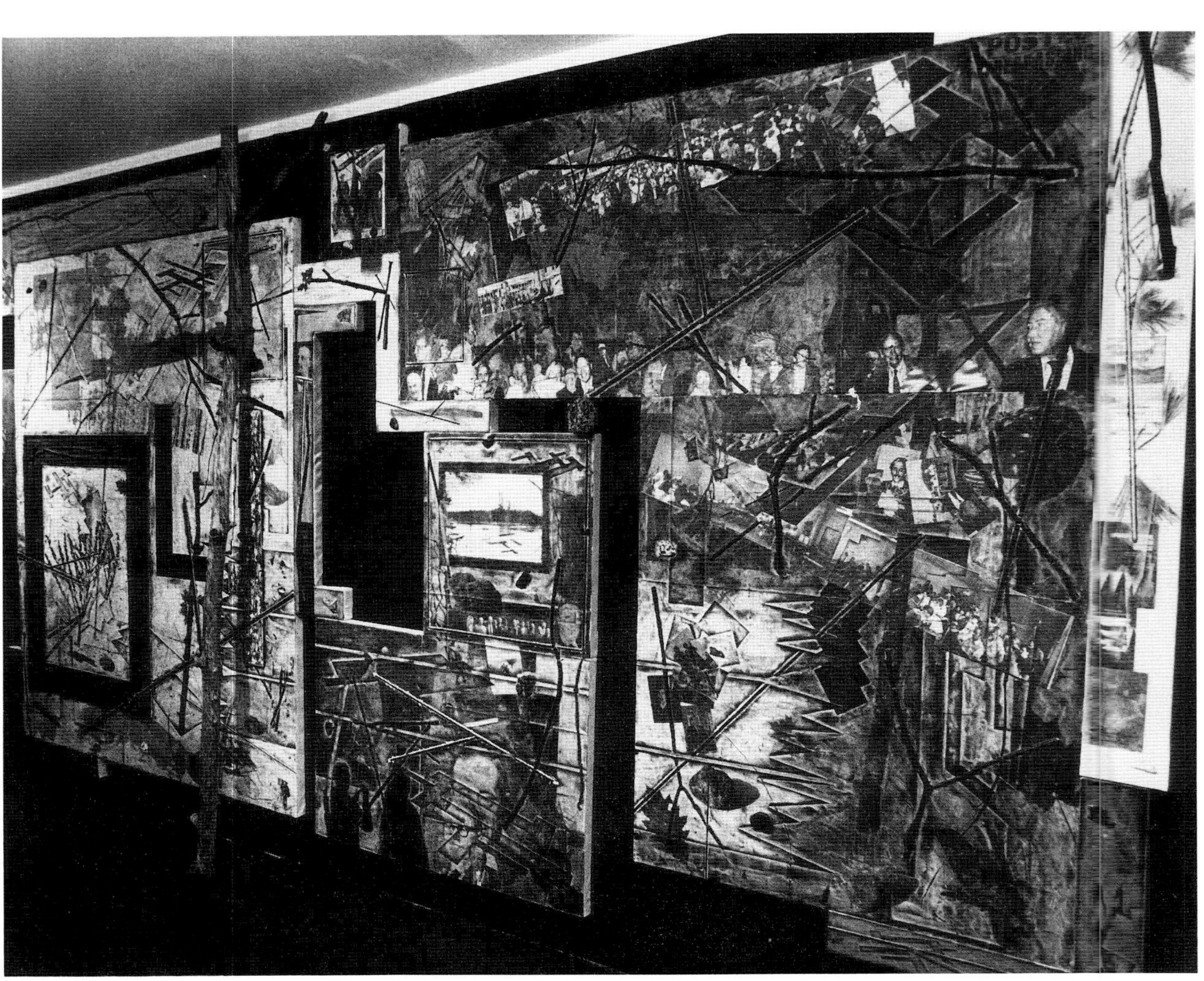

archical, these shadow images are like "litter" from the natural and social world. As witness to the current strife engendered by Governor Mario Cuomo's Commission on the Adirondacks in the 21st Century (the controversial 1990 report on the region's future), Owen deploys the political "fallout" from the numerous regional meetings held to discuss the report's provisions and its impact on the lives of Adirondackers. Through its dense and conflicting references to the natural past and the social present, Owen extends the organic processes of decay and decomposition into the political sphere. This post-modern layering of the ideas of conflict and disintegration and the resulting pictorial reintegration (albeit fragmentary and elusive) affords literal and figurative grounds for reflection upon the human condition and the state of the world in the late 20th century. In this centennial year of the legislation leading to the creation of the Adirondack Park, Americans still anxiously confront the problems posed by the deep physical and psychological cleavage between the idea of the autonomous self and an objectified natural world. Documenting the painful trajectory of our collective disconnection from the land, Owen's attempt to shape a new cultural ecology through the pictorial reintegration of man, nature and politics holds renewed promise for the second Adirondack century.

ROBERT L. McGRATH

Professor of Art History

Dartmouth College

Fig.18

FRANK OWEN
The Floor of the Forest
1990
Acrylic on canvas
102 x 294
Courtesy of Frank Owen
and Nancy Hoffman
Gallery
Photo provided by
Press-Republican.

NOTES

[1] The quote, taken from a *New York Times* editorial of 9 August, 1864, reads in full: "Within an easy day's ride of our great city, as steam teaches us to measure distance, is a tract of country fitted to make a Central Park for the world." For a discussion of the first railroad into the Adirondacks and the *New York Times* editorial see Philip G. Terrie, *Forever Wild: Environmental Aesthetics and the Adirondack Forest Preserve* (Philadelphia, 1985), pp. 92-93.

[2] For an excellent discussion of the relationship between wilderness and the metropolis, see Kenneth Myers, *The Catskills: Painters, Writers, and Tourists in the Mountains 1820-1895* (Exhibition Catalogue, The Hudson River Museum, 1987). See especially Chapter 1, "The History of Landscape Taste," pp.17 ff.

[3] See the seminal study of Barbara Novak, *Nature and Culture: American Landscape and Painting 1825-1875* (New York, 1980) for a useful discussion of the Romantic view of nature.

[4] For additional perspectives on the role of the Adirondacks in American cultural life, see *Forever Wild: The Adirondack Experience* (Exhibition Catalogue, Katonah Museum of Art, 1991).

[5] Ibid. See especially Robert L. McGrath, "The Space of Morality: Death and Transfiguration in the Adirondacks," pp. 16 ff.

[6] On the significance of the facts and legends of the Jane McCrea story see Samuel Y. Edgerton, Jr., "Asher B. Durand's Painting, 'The Murder of Miss McCrea' and Vattemare's 'System of International Exchange,'" in *The Bulletin of the Fort Ticonderoga Museum*, XI, 1965, 336-42 and "The Murder of Jane McCrea: The Tragedy of an American Tableau d'Histoire," *Art Bulletin*, XXXXVII, 1965, 481-495.

[7] For an excellent discussion of the process of landscape acculturation, see Roland Van Zandt, *The Catskill Mountain House* (New Brunswick, N.J., 1966), pp. 22 ff.

[8] Novak, op. cit., pp. 3-44 for a recent discussion of the "sublime" in American 19th century painting.

[9] For a thorough analysis of Ingham's *The Great Adirondack Pass* and other paintings from the Adirondack Museum, see Patricia C. F. Mandel, *Fair Wilderness: American Paintings in the Collection of the Adirondack Museum* (Blue Mountain Lake, N.Y., 1990), p. 73.

[10] On the Natural History Survey, see Terrie, op. cit., 27 ff.

[11] Cole had visited Lake George during the summer of 1826 to see, in his friend Cooper's words,

the "country which lies between the headwaters of the Hudson and the adjacent lakes" and to make sketches for his numerous paintings on the subject of *The Last of the Mohicans*. On these paintings see Elwood C. Perry III, *The Art of Thomas Cole: Ambition and Imagination* (Newark, N.J., 1988), pp. 47-67. A trip to Schroon Lake in the fall of 1835 was followed by the visit of June 24, 1837, in the company of Durand. The major source for Cole's Adirondack trips is Louis Legrand Noble, *The Life and Works of Thomas Cole* (Cambridge, Mass., 1964), pp. 176 ff. See also Joseph Amarotico, "Thomas Cole in the Adirondacks," *Adirondack Life*, XXX, 1978, 32 ff.

[12] Cited in Terrie, op. cit., p. 32.

[13] For Stoddard's photograph of Indian Pass, see Maitland C. De Sormo, *Seneca Ray Stoddard, Versatile Camera Artist* (Saranac Lake, N.Y., 1972), p. 76.

[14] Cited in Terrie, op. cit., 52.

[15] Ibid.

[16] On Cole's recently "discovered" *Garden of Eden*, see Doreen Bolger and Kathleen Motes Bennewitz, "Thomas Cole's Garden of Eden," *Antiques* CXXXVIII (1990), 105 ff.

[17] See Mandel, op. cit., p. 59, for Longfellow's poem "The Golden Sunset" which contains the lines:
And which is earth and which the heavens
The eye can scarcely tell.

[18] Cited in Alice Cook Brown, "Charles Louis Heyde, Painter of Vermont Scenery," *Antiques* CI (1972), 1025.

[19] See Linda S. Ferber and William H. Gerdts, *The New Path: Ruskin and the American Pre-Raphaelites* (Exhibition Catalogue, The Brooklyn Museum, 1985). See also *Poetic Localities, Photographs of Adirondacks, Cambridge, Crete, Italy, Athens: William J. Stillman* (New York, 1988).

[20] In Stillman's *Autobiography of a Journalist* (Boston, 1901), p. 198, the artist wrote, "under the stimulus, in part, of the desire for something out of the ordinary line of subjects for pictures, and in part from the hope that going into the 'desert' might quicken the spiritual faculties. . . . I decided to pass the next summer [1854] in the great primeval forest of the northern part of New York State." In the same text (p. 116) he commented on the relationship between art and nature: ". . . I received from it [Ruskin's *Modern Painters*] a stimulus to nature worship, to which I was already too much inclined which made ineffaceable the confusion in my mind between nature and art."

21 Terrie, op. cit., ch. IV for an excellent account of Murray's "Fools" and the rise of landscape tourism.

22 Cited in Maitland C. De Sormo, *The "Murray Rush" in Retrospect or With the Multitudes in the Adirondacks* (Saranac Lake, N.Y., 1989), p. 93.

23 Terrie, op. cit., ch. V.

34 Ibid.

25 From *Harper's New Monthly Magazine* (1878). Reprinted in Nicolai Cikovsky, Jr. and Michael Quirk, *George Inness* (New York, 1985), p. 205.

26 See Lewis Mumford's seminal book, *The Brown Decades, A Study of the Arts in America, 1865-1895* (New York, 1931). For a recent provocative essay on Tonalism's "Twilight" sense of tragedy, see Bram Dijkstra, "The High Cost of Parasols: Images of Women in Impressionist Art," in Patricia Trenton and William Gerdts, *California Light, 1900-1930* (Exhibition Catalogue, Laguna Art Museum, 1990), pp. 33 ff.

27 See Elizabeth Gilbert Martin, *Homer Martin: A Remembrance* (New York, 1904), p. 20.

28 For example, later in life and under the influence of Darwin, the painter William James Stillman's attitude toward nature underwent a transformation. In his *Autobiography* (p. 36), he wrote during an Adirondack camping trip: "I hoped to find new subjects for art, spiritual freedom, and a closer contact with the spiritual world—something beyond the material existence. I was ignorant of the fact that art does not depend on subject, nor spiritual life on isolation from the rest of humanity, and I found what a correct philosophy would have told me . . . nature with no suggestion of art, and the dullest form of intellectual and spiritual existence" (quoted in *Poetic Localities,* p. 26, n. 5). In a well-known late 19th century travel book, Charles Dudley Warner gave voice to similar sentiments: "I had read of the soothing companionship of the forest, the pleasure of the pathless woods. But I thought, as I stumbled along in the dismal actuality, that if I ever got out of it I would write a letter to the newspapers exposing the whole thing. There is an impassive, stolid brutality about the woods that has never been enough insisted on." Charles Dudley Warner, *In the Wilderness* (Boston, 1878; repr., Blue Mtn. Lake and Syracuse, N.Y., 1990), p. 20.

29 *John Marin by John Marin*, ed. Cleve Gray (New York, n.d.), p. 110.

30 *The Selected Writings of John Marin*, ed. Dorothy Narman (New York, 1949), p. 123.

31 *John Marin by John Marin*, p. 35.

32 Like many Americans before him Weston equated the wilderness with freedom. See the artist's autobiography, *Freedom in the Wild: A Saga of the Adirondacks* (St. Hubert's,

N.Y., 1971), for an account of the years spent in an isolated cabin at St. Huberts. In an essay entitled "A Painter Speaks," *Magazine of Art*, XII (1939), 19, Weston wrote: "A semi-pantheism, sentimental though genuine, permeated my thinking: the tree, cloud, mountain, life and the eternal seen through the incandescence of the moment... I was trying to paint what I felt rather than what I saw." For an excellent introduction to the Modernist cult of nature see *The Expressionist Landscape* (Exhibition Catalogue, Birmingham Museum of Art, 1988).

33 In his autobiography *This Is My Own* (New York, 1940), p. 221, Kent wrote: "We loved our Adirondack world; its intemperate seasons; its days and nights; its skies; its sun and moon and stars and northern lights; its sounds—books, falling rain, the wind in the trees, the frogs, the myriad little insect sounds at night—its gentle sounds; its quietness; its peace."

34 From Kent's autobiography *This Is My Own*. Quoted in Mandel, op. cit., p. 80.

35 On Stettheimer's sources and subjects see Parker Tyler, *Florine Stettheimer, A Life in Art* (New York, 1963).

36 On *Bolton Landing* see Louis Finkelstein, "The Light of de Kooning," *Art News* LXI (1967), 30. Also Fig. 26 in *Carnegie Institute Museum of Art, Pittsburgh International Series* (Pittsburgh, 1979).

37 For Frankenthaler's *Bolton Landing* see John Elderfield, *Helen Frankenthaler* (New York, 1989), plate 21. See also Barbara Rose, *Frankenthaler* (New York, 1971), p. 260 for a photograph of the artist painting at Bolton Landing.

38 Elderfield, op. cit., p. 116.

39 Reproduced in Helen A. Cooper, *Winslow Homer Watercolors* (New Haven, 1986), fig. 180. Nicolai Cikovsky, Jr., *Winslow Homer* (New York, 1990), p. 109, quotes a writer in *Harper's Weekly* in 1891: "The public mind has been thoroughly aroused to the peril that threatens the Adirondack woods." See also Terrie, op. cit., pp. 93 ff. for a more detailed account of the logging crisis in the Adirondacks.

40 See *Wilderness Solitude: A Collection of New Paintings by Allen Blagden* (Exhibition Catalogue, Mongerson-Wunderlich Galleries, New York and Adirondack Museum, Blue Mountain Lake, N.Y., 1988), p. i. and fig. 7.

41 Reproduced in Albert Ten Eyck Gardner, *Winslow Homer* (New York, 1961), p. 205.

42 See, for example, *The Bridle Path* of 1868. Reproduced in John Wilmerding, *Winslow Homer* (New York, 1971), plate 14.

A Wild Sort of Beauty:
Public Places and Private Visions

Checklist of the Exhibition

All dimensions are in inches, height precedes width.

1.   ALLEN BLAGDEN

The Broad Axe, ca. 1986

Watercolor on paper, 40 x 25

Courtesy of Mongerson-Wunderlich Galleries, Chicago, Illinois.

2.   DEWITT CLINTON BOUTELLE

The Sacandaga River at Hadley, New York, 1867

Oil on canvas, 20 x 30

Adirondack Museum (90.002.01).

3.   ALFRED THOMPSON BRICHER

Untitled: Boating Party on Lake George, ca. 1867

Oil on canvas, 26 x 48

Adirondack Museum (82.004.01).

4.   FREDERIC EDWIN CHURCH

Sunrise in the Adirondacks, 1866

Oil on canvas stretched over panel, 12 1/2 x 19 1/2

Private Collection, New York, New York.

5.   SAMUEL COLMAN

Untitled: AuSable River, ca. 1869

Oil on canvas, 30 x 40

Adirondack Museum, Gift of Harold K. Hochschild (72.160.03).

6.   EDITH M. COOK

Lake Placid at Twilight, 1868

Oil on canvas, 8 3/4 x 18

Courtesy of Hood Museum of Art, Dartmouth College, Hanover, New Hampshire,

Purchased through the Julia L. Whittier Fund (P.960.61).

7.   ASHER B. DURAND

The Murder of Miss McCrea, ca. 1839

Oil on board, 12 1/2 x 17 5/8

Courtesy of Fort Ticonderoga Museum (FT-9.76).

8. HELEN FRANKENTHALER
    Bolton Landing, 1960
    Pen and gouache on paper, 19 1/4 x 12 1/8
    Collection of the artist.

9. SANFORD ROBINSON GIFFORD
    A Twilight in the Adirondacks, 1864
    Oil on canvas, 24 x 26
    Adirondack Museum (63.124.02).

10. REGIS FRANCOIS GIGNOUX
    Log Road in Hamilton County, 1844
    Oil on canvas, 27 x 34
    Adirondack Museum, Gift of Mrs. Boris Sergievsky (64.005.01).

11. CHILDE HASSAM
    Early Summer, Lake George, ca. 1900
    Watercolor on paper, 15 x 22
    Courtesy of Frederic Remington Art Museum (66.126).

12. CHARLES HEYDE
    Shelburne Point at Sunset, n.d.
    Oil on canvas, 15 x 25
    Courtesy of Dr. and Mrs. Herbert A. Durfee, Jr.

13. WINSLOW HOMER
    Casting, "A Rise", 1889
    Watercolor on paper, 9 x 20
    Adirondack Museum (67.058.01).

14. CHARLES CROMWELL INGHAM
    The Great Adirondack Pass, Painted on the Spot, 1837
    Oil on canvas, 48 x 40
    Adirondack Museum, Gift of Mr. and Mrs. Harold Grout (66.114.01).

15. AMY WISHER JONES
    St. Regis Reservation, 1937
    Oil on masonite, 28 x 53
    Adirondack Museum (86.065.01).

16. AMY WISHER JONES
    Untitled: Skater, 1937
    Watercolor on paper, 11 x 14
    Adirondack Museum, Gift of Mrs. Lynn Boillot (87.047.07).

17. AMY WISHER JONES
     Untitled: Skier, 1937
     Watercolor on paper, 11 x 14
     Adirondack Museum, Gift of Mrs. Lynn Boillot (87.047.12).

18. JOHN FREDERICK KENSETT
     Lake George, 1856
     Oil on canvas, 26 x 42
     Adirondack Museum (65.079.01).

19. ROCKWELL KENT
     At Peace, 1940
     Oil on canvas, 28 x 40
     Courtesy of D. Wigmore Fine Art, Inc., New York, New York.

20. EMANUEL GOTTLIEB LEUTZE
     Indians and American Captive, ca. 1862
     Oil on canvas, 17 x 25
     Adirondack Museum (65.028.01).

21. JONAS LIE
     Men's Camp and Stables, 1930
     Oil on canvas, 30 x 45
     Adirondack Museum, Gift of Mrs. Francis P. Garvan (76.217.03).

22. GEORGE LUKS
     Mountain Stream, 1931
     Watercolor on paper, 14 x 20 1/4
     Courtesy of Munson-Williams-Proctor Institute, Museum of Art,
          Utica, New York (58.297).

23. JOHN MARIN
     Fulton Chain, Adirondacks, No. 2, 1912
     Watercolor on paper, 13 3/4 x 16 1/4
     Adirondack Museum (91.023.001).

24. HOMER DODGE MARTIN
     Lake Sanford, 1870
     Oil on canvas, 24 1/2 x 39 1/2
     Courtesy of The Century Association (1873.3)

25. HOMER DODGE MARTIN

Iron Mine, Port Henry, New York, ca. 1862

Oil on canvas, 30 1/8 x 50

Courtesy of National Museum of American Art, Smithsonian

    Institution, Gift of William T. Evans (1910.9.11).

26. DON NICE

Adirondack Totem, 1990

Oil on canvas, 80 x 43

Collection of the artist.

27. GEORGIA O'KEEFFE

Maple and Cedar (Red) Lake George, 1923

Oil on canvas, 25 x 20

Collection of Mr. and Mrs. Gerald P. Peters, Santa Fe, New Mexico (B-6906).

28. FRANK OWEN

The Floor of the Forest, 1990

Acrylic on canvas, 102 x 294

Courtesy of Frank Owen and Nancy Hoffman Gallery.

29. LEVI WELLS PRENTICE

Smith's Lake, Adirondacks, N.Y., 1883

Oil on canvas, 26 x 48

Adirondack Museum, Gift of Mr. and Mrs. Harold K. Hochschild (66.023.02).

30. FREDERIC SACKRIDER REMINGTON

Spring Trout Fishing in the Adirondacks - An Odious Comparison of Weights, 1890

Monochrome oil on canvas, 22 x 30

Adirondack Museum (70.196.01).

31. WILLIAM TROST RICHARDS

In the Adirondacks, 1857

Oil on canvas, 29 x 44

Adirondack Museum (69.053.01).

32. JULIAN RIX

Adirondack Landscape, ca. 1900

Oil on canvas, 18 x 26

Courtesy of Frederic Remington Art Museum (66.127).

33. HORACE WOLCOTT ROBBINS, JR.
Untitled: Wolf Jaw Mountain, 1863
Oil on canvas, 13 x 22
Adirondack Museum (74.292.01).

34. FREDERIC RONDEL
A Hunting Party in the Woods./In the Adirondac [sic], *N.Y. State*, 1856
Oil on canvas, 22 x 30
Adirondack Museum, Gift of The Shelburne Museum,
Shelburne, Vermont (65.015.01).

35. JAMES DAVID SMILLIE
After Showers, Keene Valley, N.Y., n.d.
Oil on canvas, 24 1/2 x 40 1/2
Courtesy of Danforth Museum of Art Collection,
Gift of Dr. Cynthia Starr Endick and Kenneth J. Endick
in honor of Dr. Benjamin Starr (1986.34).

36. JAMES DAVID SMILLIE
Top of Giant's Leap, Adirondacks, 1869
Watercolor on paper, 20 x 13
Adirondack Museum, Gift of Mrs. Harold K. Hochschild (62.009.01).

37. FLORINE STETTHEIMER
Lake Placid, 1919
Oil on canvas, 40 x 50
Courtesy of Museum of Fine Arts, Boston. Gift of
Miss Ettie Stettheimer, the artist's sister (47.1541).

38. WILLIAM JAMES STILLMAN
Saranac Lake, Adirondack Mountains, 1854
Oil on canvas, 30 1/2 x 25 1/2
Courtesy of Museum of Fine Arts, Boston. Gift of Dr. J. Sydney Stillman (1977.842).

39. ARTHUR FITZWILLIAM TAIT
A Good Time Coming, 1862
Oil on canvas, 20 x 30
Adirondack Museum, Gift of Harold K. Hochschild (63.037.01).

40. ELIPHALET TERRY
Baker's Farm, 1859
Oil on canvas, 19 x 30
Anonymous.

41. JACOB C. WARD
    Outlet of Lake George, ca. 1840
    Oil on canvas, 21 3/4 x 30
    Courtesy of Memorial Art Gallery of the University of Rochester;
    Marion Stratton Gould Fund (47.19).

42. HAROLD WESTON
    Birch Tree, 1922
    Oil on canvas, 22 x 16
    Collection of Nina Weston Foster.

43. HAROLD WESTON
    Clouds—Upper Ausable Lake, 1922
    Oil on canvas, 16 x 20
    Collection of Nina Weston Foster.

44. GUSTAVE ADOLF WIEGAND
    Blue Mountain, ca. 1914
    Oil on canvas, 41 x 48
    Adirondack Museum, Gift of Mrs. Paul R. Tilson, artist's daughter (73.043.79).

45. FERDINAND ALEXANDER WUST
    Early Morning in the Adirondacks: The Successful Hunter, 1873
    Oil on canvas, 74 x 48
    Adirondack Museum (81.045.01).

46. ALEXANDER HELWIG WYANT
    Adirondack Vista, ca. 1881
    Oil on canvas, 25 x 19
    Adirondack Museum, Gift of Walter Hochschild (74.294.01).

47. DON WYNN
    Campfire, 1975
    Oil on canvas, 90 x 72
    Adirondack Museum, Gift of Mr. and Mrs. J. Richardson Dilworth (82.085.02).

LIST OF IMAGES